AF469760

CRIME AND THE ART MARKET

CRIME AND THE ART MARKET

Riah Pryor

LUND HUMPHRIES

First published in 2016 by

Lund Humphries

16 St Martin's Le Grand
London
EC1A 4EN
UK

www.lundhumphries.com

ISBN Hardback: 978-1-84822-171-0
ISBN eBook (PDF): 978-1-84822-190-1
ISBN eBook (ePUB): 978-1-84822-189-5
ISBN eBook (mobi): 978-1-84822-203-8

A Cataloguing-in-Publication record for this book is available from the British Library.

Designed by Crow Books
Printed and bound in Croatia by Imago

CONTENTS

PREFACE

The first time I stood in an auction house as a journalist, I presumed that every art dealer and collector around me was a suspect waiting to happen. After a few years working as a reseracher in the Art & Antiques Unit of London's Metropolitan Police Service (at New Scotland Yard), my perspective on the art market was cynical, to say the least.

Readers of mainstream coverage on the subject of art crime will hear the art market described as 'murky' and 'unregulated', and may similarly share such cynicism. But how accurate, or fair, is this presumption of the art market being 'guilty until proven innocent'? It did not take many more years working as a journalist within the art market for my early views to be challenged. Despite my ongoing interest in reporting on criminal and civil cases involving art works, with every specialist dealer and passionate collector I met, the complexity of the reasons behind art crime became obvious.

This book is an attempt to outline where my opinions are today. There is more at stake than simply determining how many criminals there are in the art market. Under consideration are concerns as to whether the art market, with its opaque structures and secretive ways of doing business, is fundamentally facilitating criminal activity.

To pick the situation apart, one must delve into an intricate network of political, financial, ethical and personal factors, and consider how art crime functions within the market. The extent to which attempts to investigate and prevent the problem compare to other sectors within society also needs to be examined. These tasks equally demand an appreciation of the fact that the art market itself has changed exponentially since study of art crime began.

If misunderstanding is a worrying foundation to begin a book, it would have been far more so, were it not for my friend and former editor, Melanie Gerlis. My ability to write anything substantial on this subject is thanks to everyone at *The Art Newspaper*, particularly Georgina Adam, and my former colleagues at New Scotland Yard. The following are also thanked for their advice and insights on this project: Lucy Myers and Lund Humphries, Karen Sanig, Janet Ulph, Martin Wilson, Kenneth Polk, Bojan Dobovšek, Melanie McFadyean, Anthony Browne, Pierre Valentin, Chris Marinello, Nicholas Brett, Robert Read, Julian Radcliffe, Adriano Picinati di Torcello, Leila A. Amineddoleh, Joe Hill, Judith Prowda and Matthew Paton. Of course, thanks also go to my family (the Pryors and the Palmers) and husband Rob – to whom this book is dedicated.

Introduction

CALLS FOR CHANGE

A criminal's playground?

As the familiar proverb says: 'One bad apple spoils the barrel.' A 2005 survey considering the impact of new legislation on the antiquities market found that 36 per cent of respondents working in the trade believed the problem of looted antiquities being sold on the art market could be attributed to 'bad apples'. In other words, it was felt that a small sector of the trade was misbehaving and giving the broader sector a bad reputation. Those conducting the survey were unconvinced:

> we suggest that this represents a somewhat pious and complacent view on the part of dealers who may well themselves be dealing in illicit antiquities, perhaps unwittingly.[1]

Opinions on the art market and its relationship with criminal activity have not improved since. The US-based economist Professor Nouriel Roubini declared at the 2015 Davos World Economic Forum that regulation was needed in the art market to prevent its exploitation by criminals, reportedly describing how the sector 'had weaknesses that would not be allowed in other kinds of financial markets, such as equities'.[2] The comments sparked debate across the globe: had the sector been allowed to follow its own rules, unwatched, for too long?

Concerns about trade in cultural property and the degree to which the market accommodates criminal activity are in line with broader international discussions around the need for stronger scrutiny of markets in high-risk assets. The political climate for greater transparency and regulation has been accelerating since the social, economic and political upheaval following the 2008 global financial crisis. As societies worldwide feel the hit of subsequent economic measures and the gap between the rich and the poor increases, governments are feeling public pressure to act on issues that are more traditionally linked to the upper echelons of society – notably tax evasion, money laundering and corruption.

It is unsurprising that the art market is facing a share of this criticism. The seemingly subjective financial value of cultural property has long proved a hurdle for tighter rules around the art trade, and the stratospheric leaps in prices at the top end of the market, which have risen over the US$100 million mark in recent years (including the sale of Pablo Picasso's *Les Femmes d'Alger, Version 'O'* (1955) at Christie's, New York, for $179 million in May 2015), has boosted feeling that the art world is not grounded in any objective value system or set of controls. Add to this complex and fluid value system an unprecedented expansion of cross-border trade in art and an ongoing lack of transparency, and it is unsurprising that opportunities for criminal activity in the market appear rife. The seeming proliferation of criminal cases involving forgeries, looted antiquities and the circulation of stolen art in recent years further supports speculation that the industry is in need of greater controls.

This book considers a key question emerging from the image of the art trade as 'murky': Is the market a criminal's playground, open to illicit activity and providing an environment where good and bad apples are one and the same?

SCOPE

A typical reaction to telling someone that you work in the field of art crime goes a little like this: 'Wow, that sounds interesting . . . what exactly is that?'

The scope of the topic is broad. Most commonly, however, coverage of art crime is dominated by forgeries, stolen art, criminal damage against art and the looting of antiquities. However, the use of art in crime also extends to bribery, tax evasion, money laundering and so-called 'white-collar crimes' (although definitions vary, it can be understood as crimes conducted by persons in business or positions of authority who abuse their position), including anti-trust violations and financial manipulations, such as embezzlement.[3]

These offences can loosely be organised into the following categories: art as the target for criminal activity (i.e. theft and forgery); art used within crime (where the work of art played a pivotal role within the criminal act, but was part of a broader criminal act, for example in use as collateral within a network trading in drugs); and crimes against art (i.e. vandalism against art). A fourth category, art as a criminal act, can be used to describe works of art that are deemed to be criminal acts themselves (e.g. art investigated as being 'obscene' in terms of its content).

Not all of the cases, disputes and investigations mentioned within this book will have been resolved in a criminal court. There are numerous reasons – evidential, political and financial – why situations which could be deemed criminal are not resolved in court. Therefore, if the original conduct could be considered criminal, it is included in the discussion in this book, regardless of how the dispute was resolved. Acts that are unlawful but not necessarily covered by criminal law are also included as a means to explore market practices.

In terms of the objects involved in art crime, a divide in discussion is often apparent between those primarily concerned with archaeological items (including art made in past civilisations) under threat from looting, destruction or illicit export, and those concerned with fine art, where focus falls on forgeries, intentional damage and theft. The terminology used to describe objects in this topic is varied: the term 'cultural property' is increasingly being dropped in favour of 'cultural heritage' (see Chapter 5), while the use of the term 'art' in discussion of 'art crime' tends to neglect the breadth of heritage at stake (e.g. buildings, archival material).

This book indulges in a broad scope, using its focus on the market as a means to assume that if the art trade would deal in the property, it should be included in discussion here. The terms art, cultural property and cultural heritage are all used but understood as relating to items 'being sold in the art market' (rather than alternative definitions of the terms held by other sources). The exception to this scope is immoveable culture attacked in situ, notably buildings or monuments, which are also considered.

This broad scope in terms of objects is partly an acknowledgement that if we are examining criminal activity within the market, the market itself should form the natural boundary of discussion. Framing discussion around the art market, rather than the type of objects involved, echoes the approach of police investigations into art crime, which are focused on the evidence available. For example, whether someone is arrested for handling a 19th-century Impressionist landscape or a 300 BCE coin will be of minor importance to the chances of prosecution (although the type of object will impact the investigation in other ways – for example, it will be more challenging to determine a clear provenance for a coin than for a painting with an auction history). Likewise, the price of items is not the deciding factor of their inclusion in this book. There is a natural tendency to give greater attention to high-value items affected by art crime, but it is often the lower-level crimes committed on a mass volume that create the most damage to a market and broader society.

Focusing on the art market rather than the broader 'art world' does not automatically limit discussion to the actions of auction houses, dealers, collectors and art advisers, nor does it exclude non-profit institutions and their professionals (e.g. museums and art historians). Rather, it acknowledges that the latter participate in transactions within the art market and that many art-based professions are increasingly interchangeable: collectors often work in museums, dealers often possess the same expertise in their subject of choice as those working in cultural institutions.

One limiting factor is geography. The UK and the US are the dominant areas of investigation here. This limit exists partly because of the size of the publication, but it also represents my own professional experience and the fact that much of the art market continues to flow from these centres. As the art market is international and relies on cross-border trade, the discussion still includes other countries' systems of enforcement and jurisdiction, but priority is given to the UK's and US's relationships with other countries, not vice versa.

A BRIEF HISTORY

Art crime is not a new problem. From grave-robbers in Ancient Egypt, to the Renaissance hero Michelangelo's attempted imitation of a faun sculpture from antiquity and the 1911 theft of Leonardo da Vinci's *Mona Lisa*: art's relationship with crime is as old and ever-changing as culture itself.

The historical trajectory of art crime differs widely in distinct sections of the art market (e.g. in the trade of Old Master paintings compared to contemporary art), geographic regions and the type of offence (e.g. theft versus fraud). However, two major lines of development can be said to have shaped criminal activity in this field.

The first was the widespread conceptualisation of '[the] artist as genius', which developed during the Renaissance [period]. No longer was the creator of a work simply the master craftsman of a workshop; an artist's input bestowed an additional value onto the piece itself. This 'aura' of the artist and the simultaneous consolidation of the concept of the 'original' (i.e. a work by a particular 'artist' understood as being superior to that of another, or a copy) laid the foundation for today's concerns with the 'authentic'. From a criminal perspective, the concept of an original came with its own deliciously sweet development: there was now an even more profitable target to chase and a way to make money.

Money, unsurprisingly, is the second key development, or rather the attachment of monetary values to cultural goods. By the 17th century, a system of dealers and private auctioneers had been established. From that century onwards, Grand Tours around Europe by the upper classes provided easy markets for forgers and looters alike to offload their wares.

The growth of US buyers entering Europe's art market at the beginning of the 20th century continued to inspire criminals, who proved as keen to target these well-heeled buyers as the legitimate dealers were. As London and New York emerged as the dominant centres for art sales in the 1960s, a wave of thefts (including along a strip of the French Riviera) suggested that criminal activity was equally picking up pace. By the 1970s, as the art market began its boom, art thefts accelerated: Italian museums reported the loss of over 3,000 works of art in 1971 alone.[4] Law enforcement was increasingly equipping itself for the fight against art crime, including the creation of the Metropolitan Police Service's Art & Antiques Unit in 1969.[5] Pressure to stem the sale of looted antiquities also began to build, as the international community began to wake up to the burgeoning black market.

A more systematic interest in art crime came from academics and media in the 1990s, partly due to the swell of Holocaust restitution cases and a cluster of headline-grabbing thefts: 20 paintings, stolen from Amsterdam's Van Gogh Museum in 1991 and later abandoned; the infamous (and still unresolved) theft of art worth an estimated $500 million from the Boston's Isabella Stewart Gardner Museum in 1990; Edvard Munch's *The Scream* (1893), stolen from Oslo's National Gallery in 1994; and the conviction of prolific UK art forgers John Myatt and John Drewe in 1999, for creating and selling more than two hundred forgeries. The expansion of the art market since 2000 has opened up further transnational opportunities for criminals, with a concurrent concern from the international community that cultural property could be used within broader organised and cross-border crime (e.g. terrorism).

Plotting the evolution of art crime alongside the development of the market alone does, however, neglect the impact of political and social watersheds. The prime example is the Second World War, which resulted in the destruction and looting of cultural property on a scale unprecedented in modern history. The number of Nazi art crimes continues to shock: more than 25,000 looted artworks are currently on a Central

Registry of Information of Looted Cultural Property,[6] and an estimated third of all art privately owned in France was lost.[7] Today, concern over the loss of cultural heritage embroiled in conflicts in the Middle East continues to demonstrate that art crimes, set within broader moments of political and social upheaval, can prove the greatest prompt to efforts to tackle the issue.

A meaningful understanding of the history of art crime, its origins and society's responses has long been stumped by the lack of accurate and reliable data. The well-documented claim that US$6 billion a year is lost due to art theft appears to have derived from a figure provided by the FBI,[8] but there is no clear or detailed explanation as to how this number was reached. Equally, the often-quoted claim that art crime is the world's third most common form of trafficking (after drugs and arms trafficking) is questioned by critics who reference the international police organisation INTERPOL's online admission that:

> We do not possess any figures which would enable us to claim that trafficking in cultural property is the third or fourth most common form of trafficking, although this is frequently mentioned at international conferences and in the media.[9]

INTERPOL has attempted to gather some reliable data. Member countries are asked for statistics on theft of works of art on an annual basis. Only 60 replies, on average, are reported as being returned each year (out of 187 member countries).[10]

Given the absence of concrete data to represent the scale of art crime today, it is too simplistic to attribute growing interest in the topic solely to a rise in criminal activity. Instead, the rising coverage of the issue can be understood as part of a broader accumulating interest in the art market (due to its jaw-dropping prices), more focused academic attention to the subject and a political moment in which there is mounting interest in the behaviour and ethics of the wealthy.

MYTHS AND SHIFTS

Some of the most exciting breakthroughs in an art crime investigation are made sat at a desk, coffee in hand, a stack of papers at your side. It may be a far cry from the audacious heists depicted in fictional art crime portrayals, such as the 1999 film *The Thomas Crown Affair*, and the covert police operations that grab public attention, but trawling through intelligence reports and auction house catalogues can often be the slog required to piece evidence together.

The natural tendency to focus on adrenalin-packed chases for stolen art (typically featuring high-value works rather than the mid- to low-priced items that go missing on a wider and more frequent scale) has confused or, at least, oversimplified understanding of art crime. For example, the belief that 'Some thieves steal on commission, taking artworks that a collector agrees in advance to buy for a prearranged amount'[11] neglects the reality that burglary (often opportunistic) involving a painting amongst other household items was, and still is, a far more common (if not the most common) form of art theft.

There are, of course, criminals specialising in or targeting art: for example, the Dutch antiques dealer Cornelius M., who was reported to have commissioned robberies targeting works of art in France between 1998 and 2008;[12] the UK's Oliver Fallon, an academic convicted for stealing valuable records from archives in Edinburgh in 2006;[13] or even the numerous examples of museum employees helping themselves to exhibits on the sly. Nevertheless, repeat offenders are typically first attracted by a casual discovery that art can attract decent profit, rather than by a deep knowledge of or affinity with the property itself.

Academic research has played a crucial role in shifting thinking on art crime and providing a deeper awareness of the breadth of offences and their impacts. The seminal study by criminologist John E. Conklin – *Art Crime*, published 1994 – framed offences involving art to the social organisation of the art world. His preferred methodology, known as the 'routine-activities approach', compartmentalised the issue into considerations of target suitability (i.e. the art works), guardianship (i.e. security) and motivated offenders (and what those motivations were). These factors dominated, and continue to dominate, discussion of the topic – which is increasingly systematic and frequent, thanks to dedicated courses and conferences run by organisations such as the Association for Research into Crimes against Art (ARCA) and legal forums, notably the Institute of Art and Law.

Examination of criminal cases involving art and informed by this broader background of study has developed a new set of beliefs around the nature of art crime. First, it is broadly accepted that the majority of art crime is conducted for financial motives. Where alternative motives are discernible, they are often an additional motive to finance: for example, a composite of motives including a desire for revenge. The major exception to this rule is the attack on culture as part of a political statement or as an attack on a society's identity (e.g. the Taliban's 2001 bombing of the sixth-century Buddhas of Bamiyan, in Afghanistan).

A further shift in contemporary understanding of art crime is the clearer appreciation of the use of cultural property within broader criminal organisations. Historic instances – such as the rumoured involvement of the Sicilian mafia in the 1969 theft of a Caravaggio painting from an oratory in Palermo, and the IRA's links to the 1974 heist of paintings from the Alfred Beit collection in Ireland's Russborough House (which included works by Goya and Peter Paul Rubens) – had long highlighted art's role within wider criminal endeavours. However, it was with the wider international interest in organised, transnational crime,[14] which accelerated during the 1990s, that more systematic attention to the use of art in organised crime emerged. Today, debates about the sale of looted antiquities funding terrorist organisations dominate much of the mainstream discussion of art crime.

Greater appreciation of art's use in organised crime has added some grit to, and removed some glamour from, our understanding of art crime. It has not, however, removed scrutiny of the art market's practices and the extent to which they directly (or indirectly) aid criminal activity.

Discussions about the moment or point at which 'legitimate' and 'illicit' art markets meet are adjoined with conceptualisation of the sector as a 'grey market'. That is, items enter the market from an illicit activity and then are absorbed into the legitimate market.[15] There tends to be a tone in mainstream commentary on the art trade that some of the legal boundaries within which its professionals work are somewhat fuzzy and that even the generally well-behaved professionals working in the sector could be tempted into a little illicit activity if an enticing opportunity arose.

Any sweeping perception of the behaviour of art market players, or assumption that crimes involving art are only of concern to the wealthy, risks oversimplifying the art market itself. Rather than a cohesive, unitary sector, the trade is better understood as a series of subsectors: in terms of the objects sold, the key players involved, price points and the risks of criminal activity.

Limiting study to a particular sector of the art market could then provide a more accurate understanding. For example, a two-year study carried out by Professor of Criminology Kenneth Polk and Associate Professor Christine Alder considered authenticity issues surrounding Aboriginal art. By focusing on just one part of the art trade, the research was able to separate issues that a 'purchaser of any form of fine art' would face (e.g. determining whether a work is authentic) from issues that were specific to those purchasing art in this part of the art trade (e.g. what does it mean for a work to be authentic in the context of Aboriginal art?).[16]

Today's understanding of art crime is increasingly appreciative of the fact that the problem is grittier, more financially motivated and organised than once believed. However, some of the opinions on art crime that are evident in general coverage of the subject need further challenge: the idea that art crime only impacts the few and wealthy; the belief that the art trade exists free from any supervision or regulations; and the feeling that criminals involved in art (particularly forgers) are deserving of an admiration not offered to criminals targeting other markets. These viewpoints are considered throughout the following chapters.

UNDER ATTACK OR UNDER SUSPICION?

This book considers criminal activity linked to the art market and the extent to which the market's practices can directly, or indirectly, be held responsible for it. Does the sector need greater support or scrutiny?

Chapters have been ordered into two sections. The first half of the book focuses on the traditional 'villains'. How does criminal activity occur in, around and through today's art market, and what impact is it having?

The first chapter, 'New Opportunities for Old Tactics', considers three key factors which can encourage criminal activity around art to prosper: conflict, emerging markets for art, and technological revolutions. Adjoining case studies do not constitute an exhaustive review of art crime today, but identify environments in which art crime thrives.

The second chapter, 'A Crime of Consequence', explores the broad range of ramifications that art crime enacts upon individual victims, the art market, broader society and the perpetrators themselves. How this impact is then understood and prioritised by those advising on the regulation, prevention and enforcement against such criminal activity is considered in the third chapter, 'When Is a Problem a Problem?'.

The second section of the book will consider the 'heroes' to our 'villains' – that is, those who work to prevent, investigate and resolve cases of criminal activity in the art market. Thus, the fourth chapter, 'The Solution Sector', takes a look at the growing landscape of professionals working in this field (including lawyers, specialist detectives and recovery agents), while the following chapter, 'The Legal Landscape', provides an overview of the legislation available to carry out such work. Finally, a collation of the proposed solutions to tackling art crime is examined in the sixth chapter, 'The Next Step?'.

Separating the 'problems' from the 'solutions' in this way is arguably too simplistic: a black-and-white approach cannot comfortably discuss a market in which so much information remains under wraps. However, a flexible 'cops-and-robbers' approach should at least maintain some of the subject's original intrigue, while exploring how shifts in the market have changed the environment for crime and the extent to which the art market itself can be held responsible.

PART I

THE VILLAINS

Chapter 1

NEW OPPORTUNITIES FOR OLD TACTICS

There was a running joke in New Scotland Yard's Art & Antiques Unit. Following a successful conviction and media buzz around an art crime, we would anticipate a new 'trend' being spotted by journalists, questions emerging from academics and similar crime reports arriving.

Often, these 'trends' were simply the result of individuals reading the news and being prompted to come forward with their concerns about a painting, or police officers having developed contacts around a particular artist's work and receiving better intelligence. Similarly, once journalists are alerted to a particular area of crime in the art trade (e.g. forgeries in a particular artist's work), there tends to be a series of related stories as the media becomes better acquainted with the sector.

Exploring clusters of related crimes can, of course, be insightful. At times, it can reveal a broader criminal network. For example, a series of frauds in 2010 using fake credit cards targeting more than 40 UK-based companies (including leading auction houses) was soon uncovered by police as the work of one criminal network and, ultimately, ended in the conviction of three individuals.[1] More typically, a wave of offences within a particular sector of the art market (e.g. antiquities) reflects a broader set of risks or vulnerabilities at play (e.g. the start of conflict in a region may spur a wave of illicitly excavated objects).

This chapter explores three key factors which repeatedly crop up when studying trends (whether historical or contemporary) in art crime: conflict, emerging markets for art, and technological revolutions. These are not mutually exclusive, nor are they a comprehensive list of factors which seem to be present whenever art crime appears to be on the rise. The nature of each of these factors is also constantly changing; conflicts currently raging in the Middle East are obviously very different to those of Napoleon's day. Similarly, we have already considered how the art market itself (in general and among its subsectors) is fluid and rapidly developing. Nevertheless, where any one or more of these factors is apparent within a situation, one can expect some form of art crime to occur.

CONFLICT

It has been a reality throughout history that the ugliest side of humanity can result in the destruction and loss of its most beautiful creations. Some of the most emotive and enduring art crime cases stem from conflict: typically, through looting, destruction and theft.[2]

A glance at historical examples soon reveals the consistency of crime involving cultural heritage within war and the development of international attempts to prevent (or at least rectify the damage from) it. Judge, writer and educator Arthur Tompkins describes the 'spoils of war' attitude to looting as a 'right' or 'trophy of victory'[3] which dominated the civilisations of the classical world – the Greeks, the Romans and the Persians, in particular – and continued unabated right through to the end of the Napoleonic era. A shift away from this widespread assumption that cultural property should be amassed within any decent 'spoils of war' collection strengthened in the 19th century, with the Congress of Vienna (1814–1815), which included a call for Napoleon to return art seized during his campaigns, and with the American Civil War's Lieber Code of 1863,[4] which implemented conduct regulations for soldiers and forbade the harm and destruction of cultural property during battle. Cultural property remained on government agendas into the early 20th century, as peace treaties were drawn up following the First World War – notably in the Treaty of Versailles and the Treaty of Saint-Germain-en-Laye, both of 1919.

The sheer breadth, scale and organisation of cultural losses during the Second World War, spearheaded by Nazi looting and destruction of so-called degenerate art, was a watershed moment for the protection of culture in conflict. Not only did it prompt short-term action – notably the 1943 Inter-Allied Declaration 'to do their utmost to defeat the methods of dispossession practised by the Axis Powers and their associates against countries and peoples whom they have so wantonly assaulted and despoiled'[5] – but also, on a longer-term basis, governments acknowledged that there was an ongoing problem of cultural items being targeted whenever battle lines were drawn.

The 1954 Hague Convention for the Protection of Cultural Property in the Event of Armed Conflict represented an international commitment to protect cultural property within conflict (a 1999 protocol added some teeth to the agreement, by introducing criminal offences), while the 1977 amendment protocols to the Geneva Conventions and the 1998 Rome Statute of the International Criminal Court also recognised art within their broader consideration of humanitarian rules.

This recognition that culture is at risk within conflict was increasingly met with appreciation that attacks on heritage are used as a deliberate tactic within broader attacks on the identities of societies. The breakdown of Yugoslavia in the 1990s saw the deliberate targeting of culture associated with particular ethnic and religious groupings (discussed as a case study later in this chapter), while ideological vandalism towards art has proved a consistent feature in ongoing wars in the Middle East, including the aforementioned 2001 destruction of Afghanistan's Buddhas of Bamiyan by the Taliban, militant attacks on the ancient city of Nimrud, Iraq, in 2015 and (in the same year) the destruction of the ancient Temple of Baalshamin, in Palmyra, Syria. With reference to the latter, the Director-General of UNESCO Irina Bokova stated: 'The systematic destruction of cultural symbols embodying Syrian cultural diversity reveals the true intent of such attacks, which is to deprive the Syrian people of its knowledge, its identity and history.'[6]

The nature of contemporary conflicts is also reshaping how crime involving cultural property functions. Today's wars are discussed as often being intra-state and privatised[7] – that is, no longer necessarily between countries' governments and often featuring international players or groupings (including insurgents) who require funding via criminal networks. There is general consensus that the looting and sale of looted antiquities is one such avenue of funding, although the scale of this activity remains in debate. Certainly there are some shocking headline examples: the repeated looting of the National Museum of Afghanistan, in Kabul, in the 1990s which resulted in the loss of 70 per cent of the 100,000 objects on display, and the National Museum of Iraq, in Baghdad, in 2003, alongside reports of widespread illicit excavation of some of the world's most significant archaeological sites.

If the wealth of historical examples and ongoing threats to culture within conflict present a grim trajectory, there are signs that the protection of cultural property in times of conflict could improve. The flow of information about threats to culture is more vivid and instantaneous than ever before, with individuals now able to upload video footage of attacks on cultural institutions, property or heritage sites online and to international audiences. Naturally, citizen journalism arrives with its own complexities. It is challenging, for example, to validate the authenticity and the neutrality of uploaded footage. Online videos can also be used as a means of propaganda, as per the 2015 video clip of Islamist militants destroying artefacts in Iraq, reported to have been uploaded by ISIS (otherwise known as Islamic State, ISIL or Daesh).[8]

Contemporary developments aside, the key reasons why art crime sits so comfortably with conflict are consistent throughout history: that is, reduced law enforcement capabilities, lapsed security measures (both in cultural institutions, heritage and private buildings), the lack of adequate government resources to protect cultural property, poverty and political confusion.

CASE STUDY: THE FORMER YUGOSLAVIA

The majority of people I met in Bosnia and Herzegovina were uncomfortable talking about the conflict surrounding the breakdown of Yugoslavia in the 1990s and the resulting conflicts. It was, however, easy to find an enthusiastic account of the 2004 restoration of the Mostar Bridge.

Designed by the 16th-century Ottoman architect Mimar Hayruddin, the iconic bridge spanning the River Neretva once represented, indeed celebrated, the harmony of the multiple cultures living in the country. The subsequent destruction of the iconic structure during the brutal wars proved equally representative: this time, of the brutal divides emerging between the ethno-religious groups.

The loss of the Mostar Bridge was not the conflict's only cultural cost. In Bosnia alone, an estimated 90 per cent of the National and University Library of Bosnia and Herzegovina was destroyed,[9] substantial damage was made to the country's National Museum, while the entirety of Sarajevo's Oriental Institute was burnt down. Croatia also suffered losses, including the infamous damage to Dubrovnik during the 1991–2 siege on the city led by the Yugoslav Army. Losses of privately owned items are hard to determine but likely substantial.

A proportion of this destruction was indirect or unintended collateral, but much was intentional and systematic. A later report by the academic András J. Riedlmayer described the assault on Bosnia as being characterised by two features: the mass expulsion of civilians 'driven from their homes, robbed, raped and murdered for being of the "wrong" ethnicity and religion', and the 'the deliberate targeting and destruction of cultural, religious and historic landmarks'.[10]

On a domestic level, the respective governments were not in a position to implement protective measures for cultural property. The Creative Economy Group, in Belgrade, describes how: 'During the 1990s, there was state rule/behaviour not to announce moveable and immoveable goods . . . if [an] artwork is protected by state, [the state] should ensure financial resources for conservation and protection.'[11] Corruption's infiltration at the heart of the authorities equally muddied the waters. The central role culture played in the conflict was further revealed by the 2011 post-war arrest of Goran Hadžić, a Croatian Serb leader, which was reportedly prompted by his attempt to sell a painting believed to be by artist Amedeo Modigliani (although questions emerged over the work's history and authenticity, while Hadžić's lawyer denied his client's link to the painting[13]). The later arrest and 2014 proceedings against the former Croatian prime minister, Ivo Sanader, for corruption also involved reports of a potential €1million worth of art being seized.[14]

Despite the escalating situation, which was described in a 1993 Council of Europe report as a 'cultural catastrophe in the heart of Europe',[15] and the evident breaching of the 1954 Hague Convention's principles, it became apparent that international legal tools in place to prevent the destruction of cultural property were more problematic to apply to civil wars. However, post-conflict efforts to seek justice for war crimes did recognise the attacks on culture. The International Criminal Tribunal for the former Yugoslavia (ICTY) acknowledged cultural-property-related war crimes within convictions, including those of politicians and army personnel at the highest level such as Duško Tadić, Tihomir Blaškić, Pavle Strugar, Dario Kordić and Mario Čerkez.[16] The academic Jadranka Petrovic argues that this was a significant development as, while the post-Second World War Nuremberg trials acknowledged crimes against culture, this was in a comparatively 'unsystematic manner' and did not focus on immoveable culture (unlike the ICTY).[17]

The term 'cultural genocide' was, and continues to be, used colloquially to refer to such atrocities committed against cultural heritage in times of war. Nevertheless, it was made clear during the ICTY trials that the phrase had no legal authority, with 'genocide' understood as being considered applicable to 'material' destruction. Nevertheless, the ICTY courts did concede that the war crimes against culture could be used as evidence of genocide, 'or as elements to prove the mental element of the crime of genocide'.[18]

The circumstances within conflicts which were earlier identified as conducive for crimes involving cultural heritage (namely, reduced law enforcement and security capabilities, the lack of adequate government resources to protect cultural property on the ground, poverty and political confusion) were equally apparent within the region following the conflict. Unsurprisingly, governments and enforcement agencies were preoccupied with tackling corruption and seeking justice for war crimes. While some returns of items were achieved, such as the 1,500 works of art reported to have been trucked back to Vukovar, Croatia, by the Federal Republic of Yugoslavia in 2001,[19] these were sporadic. A woman in Dubrovnik who had fled the city during the siege told me of the loss she felt upon discovering that her family Bible, which had been passed down for generations, had disappeared. When I asked whether she had any hope for its being recovered, she laughed.

Today, stolen art and looted antiquities continue to emerge out of, and travel through, the region. Professor of Security Studies at the University of Maribor, Ljubljana, Bojan Dobovšek, says: 'There have been sporadic attempts to raise the awareness of customs officials but it's still very easy to move items [including stolen art] across borders. Stolen goods tend to be from Serbia, Bosnia, Macedonia and Slovenia.'[20] A discernible pattern of art stolen from Western Europe, and later resurfacing in the Balkans, also emerged. The most obvious example of this is the famous recovery of two paintings by J.M.W. Turner, stolen in Frankfurt in 1994 while on loan from the UK's Tate Gallery, which revealed links to a Serbian gang; but there were also the Art Loss Register's recovery of a work by Piet Mondrian stolen in Rotterdam and recovered in the region in 2002, and two paintings (*Head of Horse* (1962) and *Glass and Pitcher* (1944)) by Pablo Picasso which were stolen from the Sprengel Museum in Pfaeffikon[21] in 2008 and later recovered in Serbia in 2011. The high-profile thefts of three paintings (including works by Pierre-August Renoir and Rembrandt) from the National Museum of Sweden in 2000, and of Munch's *The Scream* and *Madonna* from Oslo's Munch Museum in 2004, have also been attributed to 'Eastern European gangsters'.[22]

Many of the major recoveries of art within the region were orchestrated by recovery agents based in Western Europe, including the Art Loss Register (a private UK-based company which runs a database of stolen art) and a recovery company set up in Serbia by the former head of the Art & Antiques Unit, Richard ('Dick') Ellis, in 2011, as an extension of his UK-based Art Management Limited.[23]

While conflict and immediate post-conflict chaos can be seen as a contributing factor to the rise in thefts, the increasing organisation and focus of the authorities over the past decade could well be a reason why recoveries are being made. During a 2011 interview, Julian Radcliffe, the Art Loss Register's chairman, described the macro-political climate of the region as 'helpful' to those recovering stolen art. With local police forces tightening up and new economic opportunities emerging, namely tourism, the desire to get rid of stolen items was seemingly ever more appealing for criminals as it became apparent that 'crime is not going to be as profitable now that peace has broken out, as it was during the wars.'[24]

The plight of cultural property within the Yugoslavian conflicts and post-conflict society acts as a chilling example of the risks heritage faces in modern warfare: namely, deliberate identity destruction, the use of property within organised crime and the complications civil wars can pose to international efforts to prevent its destruction.

EMERGING MARKETS

Anyone working in the art market for a period of time will begin to feel as if it is a very small world. Standing in a room of familiar faces at an art fair, it is easy to forget that the last time you saw these people was in a different time zone. The art world's networks may be as tight as ever, but the breadth and pace of the market is running at a rate like never before.

The proliferation of international art fairs, new branches of established galleries and auction houses opening worldwide, as well as the development of online activity, have resulted in the more interlinked, cross-border and fluid art trade of today. The growth of new centres for art trade, notably in Asia, South America and Africa, has opened up a host of opportunities for the galleries and cultural institutions flocking to engage with these new markets. Unfortunately, the combination of new buyers, new rules and new products has proven equally enticing for criminals.

So how does art crime work within emerging centres of trade for art? One of the major opportunities for illicit activity derives from the fact that while that country's trade may increasingly echo the strength of art markets in established art market superpowers in terms of numbers, the country or region may not yet have a comparable depth of regulation and infrastructures. China is the prime target of such criticism (considered in more depth in the following section of this chapter), with comments similar to the *Financialist*'s 2013 assertion that: 'In general, China's art market is less regulated than the West.'[25] While there is feeling that regulations in the region are tightening, it is interesting that such a distinction in standards is recognised between the East and the West. It would appear that, despite the often-heard claim that the entire art market is unregulated, there is a level of acceptance that certain standards do exist in the UK and the US trade.

Emerging centres for the trade are developing the breadth and depth of their buyers. Some buyers are arriving from more established trading centres, such as the US and UK. These art professionals may have a detailed knowledge of every key artist and art movement on their home ground, but often have less experience of the new environment and products, making it more challenging to navigate trade within it (e.g. determining the authenticity of work by an artist they are less familiar with). Similarly, buyers based in the region where the art trade is emerging (e.g. domestic buyers in Brazil) are often entering the art market for the first time and lack the experience of what risks to be looking out for.

Forgeries, falsified provenance (to alter views of authenticity or to mask the work's prior ownership) and price manipulation are just some of the illicit tactics which have thrived on such uncertainties in the buyer. Media reports reveal how tourists were the targets of wily art criminals as early as the 1920s: one British newspaper reported in 1928 how the upcoming season of American visitors to Paris was soon to be met by 'the large army of fakers of antiques, who are throwing bait for the human fish'.[26] Similarly, criminologist John E. Conklin describes the production of fake objects in Africa in the 1990s, where 'Third World people find it easy to justify their production and sale of fake objects because the ultimate purchasers are usually wealthy Westerners who are seen as exploitative of the Third World.'[27]

The interflow of trade between emerging centres and established markets can also increase the chances of crime. Fake and looted items from developing markets can find their way on to international markets, while the use of art within trade between countries can exploit loopholes or differences in jurisdiction (e.g. the movement of art in a bid to evade tax). The economist Kenneth Rogoff has considered the use of art in moving wealth out of nations with strict capital controls, stating that 'estimates put capital flight from China at about $300 billion annually in recent years'.[28] Cases have supported this idea of art being used to move capital including the 2012 arrest of Gao Ping, a Chinese art dealer detained in Madrid for financial crimes and money laundering,[29] and the 2015 return of a Jean-Michel Basquiat painting, which had been sent to London via New York's JFK airport, with a valuation of $100 (rather than its true, somewhat meatier, $8 million price tag) and seized as part of Brazilian authorities' attempts to track the proceeds of crimes from the Brazilian banker Edemar Cid Ferreira, convicted in 2006 for money laundering.[30]

Fast growth (and subsequently big profits to be made), new buyers and less mature controls and regulations: it is unsurprising that criminal activity involving art moves as quickly as legitimate business to find its place in emerging art markets.

CASE STUDY: CHINA

Of the art markets to have shaken up the predominance of the UK and US, China is the clear winner. Following the end of Chairman Mao Zedong's leadership in 1976 and the opening up of the country's trade, the region's art market has surged. By 2011, it had superseded the US as the world's largest art economy, with 30 per cent of world sales.[31] This prominence has since dropped, but with 24 per cent of global sales in 2014 (with the US at 38 per cent, and the UK at 20 per cent[32]), it looks unlikely to surrender its prominent ranking in the near future.

The rapid acceleration of China's art market (now perhaps 'emerged' rather than emerging) has not been without its fair share of challenges and allegations of criminality. The creation of fakes and forgeries and their circulation within China's domestic market and the wider international market is a widely recognised problem. Large-scale discoveries of deception, including the reports, in 2013, that a sizeable proportion of the exhibits in the Jibaozhai Museum, in Jizhou, were fake,[33] adjoin evidence of entire factories or workshops devoted to creating reproductions (and, according to many, outright forgeries). Many forgeries are imported directly into Western markets, as with the 2009 sentencing of Christopher and Constance Breithoff, from Louisiana, for their role in selling wholesale art made in China as original works by local artists.[34]

Charges that cultural property is being used to aid corruption and bribery are also rife. Indeed, a term 'elegant bribery' was coined specifically to describe the use of art works as gifts to officials or politicians, in attempts to further careers or sway deals. Journalist Jia Guo outlines a scenario whereby fakes are introduced into this process:

> The briber first presents a forged artwork as a gift to the official being bribed, which does not violate the Chinese anti-corruption laws since such artworks have very low monetary value. Then, the official auctions the painting via an auction house. Finally, the briber attends the auction and purchases the artwork back for a very high price, as if he mistook the work for an original.[35]

The looting and sale of antiquities is another area of criminal activity burgeoning in the region. The history of looting in the country is not a new problem, Professor of Law Wang Yunxia describes how cultural property became a target for Western nations throughout the 19th century, only to then suffer throughout the violent civil war across the region in the first half of the 20th century.[36] As the economy opened up to international trade in the 1980s, the illicit digging of antiquities in China truly began to flourish and, today, the situation is widely acknowledged as severe. Customs officials at Shenzen (in Guandong province) are reported to have seized more than 30,000 artefacts over a ten-year period alone.[37]

An illicit interflow of trade in cultural property between mainland China and Western markets is apparent and seemingly facilitated via Hong Kong, known as a 'Gateway between East and West'. Hong Kong's history of British rule until 1997 resulted in the difference between its laws surrounding the trade in antiquities, and those in the mainland. Despite it being an offence to take certain antiquities into Hong Kong from Mainland China without government approval, once antiquities are in Hong Kong there are no comparable restrictions on exporting the items further afield.

Hong Kong's existence as a freeport, which offers tax advantages, has connected the region with broader concerns that free-trade zones are acting as an under-the-radar spot to avoid the eyes of authorities. Switzerland's freeports, for example, have long had a reputation within the art trade as a convenient place for art criminals to store illicitly removed antiquities or through which to pass them, in order to create a more legitimate provenance (e.g. 'from a collection in Switzerland', rather than 'from the ground in Afghanistan'). The now-notorious case of the Italian antiquities dealer Giacomo Medici, who was convicted in 2004 of receiving, illegally exporting and conspiring to traffic antiquities from Italy and out into a ready international market (via high-profile sales in Sotheby's and the eventual inclusion of numerous pieces into cultural institutions, including the J. Paul Getty Museum in Los Angeles), revealed the pivotal role that Geneva's Freeport played in storing antiquities. Subsequent EU laws have tightened up oversight of European freeports, including requirements to keep and make available inventories of stored property, but it remains to be seen whether Asia's equivalents will face similar governmental scrutiny.

An interflow of illicit trade in cultural property is also discernible from the West to the East. A string of thefts targeting Chinese artefacts and rhino horn across Europe, including the raid of 15 Asian artefacts from the Château de Fontainebleau, France in 2015,[38] sparked rumours that crimes were being commissioned in Asia. In the UK, thefts targeting Chinese artefacts from multiple cultural organisations and businesses, including the Fitzwilliam Museum, Cambridge, the Powell-Cotton Museum, Kent, Gorringes Auction House, East Sussex, and Durham University Oriental Museum, resulted in 13 UK-based men being arrested[39] (although it did not stop rumours that the items were destined for further afield). The UK-based Operation Shrewd, which was set up to review theft against such artefacts, found 'that organised criminal groups have targeted museums providing access to antiquities and artefacts valued at several million pounds' and reported that the thefts were to 'feed demand from Far Eastern and South East Asian markets for rhino and cultural property'.[40]

The Chinese government's attempts to stem the illicit trade of antiquities throughout the region have included its signing up to relevant international conventions, namely the 1995 UNIDROIT Convention, which China ratified in 1997, and the 1970 UNESCO Convention, which it accepted in 1989. The country's domestic legal tools include its Law on the Protection of Cultural Relics (revised in 2002), which refers to its Criminal Law 1997 and regulations on the sale and exchange of cultural relics, requiring officials to review cultural items being sold (although this is limited to non-state-owned artefacts). Provisional regulations put in place in 2003 regarding the administration of the auction of cultural relics also require auction lots to be audited. Punishment for looting within the country is severe, despite the death penalty for this offence having been lifted (although not in time for the three men who were reported to have been executed in 2000 for stealing Tang Dynasty murals from a museum in central Shaanxi province[41]).

There have been successful returns of looted items to China, including six terracotta figurines looted from a Han Dynasty tomb in 2003, which were consigned for sale at Sotheby's.[42] When official attempts to repatriate looted items from the West fail, private buyers in China are stepping in. In 2009, a Chinese buyer bid £27 million for two bronze sculptures owned by the late designer Yves Saint Laurent and believed to have been looted from a palace in Beijing in the 19th century. The buyer later refused to pay as a sign of patriotic protest.

Curbing corruption and illicit capital flight is high on the government's agenda. Author Michael Dutra suggests that: 'Some of the most important administrative penalty provisions in the country's Law on the Protection of Cultural Relics, 2002, [LPCR] apply to government or museum officials who abuse their positions or do not perform their duties capably.'[43] Investigations have included the 2014 probe of ex-chief of security Zhou Yongkang, reportedly accused of corruption and of having around $14.5 billion-worth of assets seized, including antiques and paintings.[44] Speculation around the authenticity of a painting purportedly by 20th-century artist Zhang Daqian allegedly given as a bribe dominated the 2010 trial of another official, head of the city's Judicial Bureau, Wen Qiang, in Chongqing (he was later sentenced to death for unrelated charges).[45] The arrest of the two managers at Integrated Fine Art Solutions company, an art transport company based in Beijing, for reportedly helping buyers avoid $1.6 million in import duties and taxes,[46] equally demonstrated the government's attention to art market practices. The proliferation of art funds in the region also appears to have slowed due to the heat of closer governmental scrutiny.

Efforts have been made to more closely regulate portals for selling art within China. Beijing's Culture and Creative Industry Development Forum was reported as having announced a crackdown on 'fake works, fake sales and fake auctions' in 2012.[47] This led to the publication of a code of good practice for China's auctioneers by the Chinese Auction Industry Association, although there remains international scepticism around the impact such efforts have made to date.

The rapid expansion of China's art market, and international demand for cultural property from the country, provide a textbook example of how criminal activity can take hold in an emerging art market. Whether attempts to tackle the issues of fraud, looting and corruption will be as rapid as the market's development in the region remains to be seen.

TECHNOLOGICAL REVOLUTIONS

At the risk of revealing my age, I can recall listening to a dial tone while logging into the Internet and then diligently logging off, so others in the building could use the landline. Today, it is a very rare occurrence for my phone or laptop not to be logged into a Wi-Fi connection.

The impact of today's digital revolution on all aspects of society is profound, widespread and still in the process of being understood. Understanding its impact on art crime is no different. We can attempt to track how criminals targeting cultural property may be exploiting new opportunities (indeed, the consideration of online selling in the following section of this chapter attempts to do just that), but the reality is that today's art crime is unlikely to be understood until time provides greater hindsight.

As with all the factors considered in this chapter (so far, conflict and emerging markets), history can, however, give us a guide. Shifts in technology may feel as if they are occurring at an unprecedented rate (and arguably they are), but there is a history of technological changes opening and closing doors for criminals targeting art: specifically through new methods of production, distribution and consumption of art.

The printing revolution of the 15th century, dubbed the 'Gutenberg revolution' after Johannes Gutenberg who introduced the printing press to Europe, created the ability to reproduce works on a mass scale for the first time. It simultaneously exposed artists to risks, as the proliferation of multiple editions soon attracted authorised and non-authorised copyists to follow suit. The German Renaissance artist Albrecht Dürer's courtroom battles with the printmaker Marcantonio Raimondi, who was accused of making unauthorised copies of the artist's work (complete with a false signature), signalled the acceleration of the fraught relationship between original and fakes in the world of limited editions, which continues today.

Over the following centuries, the mass production of prints and increase in art publishing accelerated these risks. The introduction of copyright legislation (the UK's 1734 Engraving Copyright Act and the US's Copyright Act in 1790) made early moves to protect artists' reputations and livelihoods, but failed to prevent the circulation of forgeries.

The advance of mechanical processes and the development of ready-made artists' materials throughout the 19th and 20th centuries continued to open up opportunities for art forgers, who were increasingly able to replicate works using the exact same materials and processes used by the original artist. A local British newspaper reported in 1899 on some of the unprecedented problems that mass access to art prints introduced:

> With a view of checking the growing practice of palming off as originals clever copies of water-colour drawings by celebrated painters the authorities of the Print Room at the British Museum have decided to notify students who wish to make copies of certain masters that they will not in future be allowed to take away their finished drawings unless they bear the official stamp, which is to be impressed upon them.[48]

A broader cultural rejection of mass industrial practices also attracted debate around the 'aura' of artists, notably the German philosopher Walter Benjamin's seminal text 'The Work of Art in the Age of Mechanical Reproduction' of 1936. The growing importance placed on authenticity supported the accumulating respect for the artist's hand in society and its being treasured by the art market (and, simultaneously, the criminals chasing a profit within it).

Much art produced by artists today is easier to formally replicate than that created in the past. For example, an Old Master oil painting is clearly more laborious to mimic than, say, one of Damien Hirst's Spot Paintings (which have been targeted by forgers). As artists experiment with the notion of the 'original' within their work, often allowing others in the studio to make the works, there are more opportunities to formally replicate these. The Internet (see the case study on Internet sales, in the following section of this chapter) also provides criminals with an easy-to-access and sizeable wealth of information about artists' signatures, styles and missing works.

Technological advance can close as many opportunities for art crime as it opens. Raking lights, infrared imaging (to reveal underdrawings), dendrochronology (which proves useful to date wood panel paintings and frames) and mass spectrometry (to analyse the date of pigments) are just some of the methods art historians employ to better get to know the work of individual artists. When reading the witness statements of art conservation experts employed on art forgery cases, it becomes clear just how valuable these tools can also prove to the art market, outside historical interest.

In a UK art fraud case involving works purportedly by Victorian artist John Anster Fitzgerald, numerous experts were called in to examine three paintings which had in fact been created by the British-based Robert Thwaites, who was convicted for the forgeries in 2006. The criminal's meticulous research into the ageing and materials used in original works by the artist he faked had left the respected expert from the BBC's television series *Antiques Roadshow*, Rupert Maas, and gallerist Christopher Beetles, out of pocket and in the newspapers. Inconsistencies in the paint pigments (i.e. the use of pigments which would not have been available to the supposed artist) offered valuable clues, but the range of different opinions voiced in the witness statements as to whether the works were genuine acted as a reminder that scientific analysis is still open to interpretation (and is also pretty costly).

Advances in security technology, the future of automatic recognition software on stolen art databases, and even discussion of bio-engineered DNA markers[49] to help identify art works, are some of the contemporary innovations that promise to make life for the art criminal more challenging. The instantaneous communication of stolen works to networks within the art trade and to international police forces is another reality for today's offender to contend with.

Technological advance on a global scale does more than just equip criminals and investigators with greater gadgets and tools for their ongoing bid to outsmart one another. Social innovation transforms the means by which cultural property is produced, consumed and distributed. In 1968, the International Foundation for Art Research compiled a report looking into art crimes facilitated by telephone buying; today, we are dealing with anonymous sellers on eBay; and tomorrow will bring its own challenges.

CASE STUDY: ONLINE SELLING

The first police witness statement I ever took was from a man who was in serious trouble with this wife. Serious trouble. Not only had the art print he bought on eBay cost a fairly large chunk of their savings, it had also turned out to be fake.

Fake works, illicitly looted items and stolen goods: buying art online is rife with risk and the subsequent crimes are a nightmare to investigate. To better understand the risks, it is important to understand how the art market in general is using online platforms. While there have been headline-grabbing moments, such as the $9.6 million fetched in 2012 for Edward Hopper's *October on Cape Cod* (1946) through Christie's 'LIVE' website,[50] the physical entities of the market (dealers and auction houses) remain the key selling platforms. Clare McAndrew's 2015 report for TEFAF (The European Fine Art Fair) on the worldwide art trade found that only around 6 per cent of all sales were made online and fell within the price bracket $1,000 to $50,000.[51]

Of the art sale portals solely functioning on the Internet, Artnet, Artsy, Artspace and Paddle8 have been making the strongest mark. General online auctions have also been making impressive headway in the market – notably eBay, which also joined forces with Sotheby's in 2014, and Amazon, which recently began selling art works through its site.

Despite the varying levels of success of online art market operations, there has been a normalisation of buying art on the Internet. The online trade report compiled by insurance company Hiscox in 2013 found that 'collectors at all levels buy artwork online, sight unseen, with 71% of our survey respondents saying that they had bought art this way, and 26% saying that they had spent over £50,000'.[52] Buyers face the challenge of attempting to establish the provenance of the work as well as any concerns about the authenticity, with little means to seek reassurance from the vendor's identity (i.e. is he or she an established art dealer?). To some extent, the known risks of buying online (the relative anonymity of the seller, not being able to view the work) are embraced by buyers who are keen to catch a bargain.

With risk, however, comes wrongdoing. While many buyers are lured into purchasing a painting with an unclear provenance and obscure signature by the dream of 'spotting an unknown treasure', this dream is exploited by forgers who deliberately keep descriptions of objects obscure in the hope of inviting speculation as to the work's true creator. For example, Kenneth Walton was convicted for selling a fake painting purportedly by the US artist Richard Diebenkorn and has since written a book explaining how he would find art in garage sales, add signatures and then sell works online.[53]

An environment that makes buying cultural property online a risky process is equally problematic for authorities investigating cases of criminal activity within it. The anonymity of sellers is a major challenge, as is making connections between suspects who use multiple online identities. While many Internet-based companies do keep contact information of buyers and sellers, part of this remains reliant on what they are told by the criminal. If police have suspicions that an item on the Internet was, say, stolen, a request could be made for identity details from the online company. In the UK, this could be as easy as making a request and filling in any necessary Data Protection forms. If, however, the online company or offence appears to be based in another country, court warrants could be required, alongside co-operation with law enforcement agencies in the other country.

The sheer amount of time required to pull together an online art fraud case became real for me when I attempted to collate the credit card and eBay data for a UK investigation into Grant Champkins-Howard and Lee Parker. The pair were convicted in 2010 for selling fake prints purporting to be by Banksy through eBay. The forgeries were priced below £5,000, which is a mid to low price level in relation to the overall market but profitable nevertheless, when carried out on a mass scale. As with many art crimes involving the Internet, victims were spread across the globe, creating a challenge for evidence gathering and even more problematic when establishing in which jurisdiction the original crime occurred. The pair of fraudsters each received a sentence of 12 months' jail suspended for two years, plus 240 hours' unpaid work, which felt comparable to the time it took to put together the evidence for the prosecution. They also received a five-year ban from selling anything online – although the details as to how this would be monitored were unclear.

The author Matthew Williams further notes the challenges for investigating crime online, stating that 'for a crime to be committed it must also be recognised as a crime within these temporal-spatial constraints' and 'As cybercrimes can span national boundaries and legal jurisdictions, questions over what body of law should apply complicate issues of retribution.'[54] The level of resources available to run investigations into art crime online is connected to a broader debate as to whose responsibility it is to regulate the Internet and what level of responsibility is held by online portals to monitor the items being sold through their sites. Trademark battles have explored this debate around responsibility, including the 2011 court battle between eBay and L'Oréal, which saw the cosmetics company successfully demand that listings offering fakes be blocked.

In relation to art crime, eBay are clear that they 'have an established programme in place to ensure that we have the right information to remove items from sale that cause concern . . . and pass on information [to law enforcement agencies] where there is evidence of wrongdoing',[55] but do not ultimately hold legal responsibility over the items sold. Online art-sales platforms for major auction houses, such as Sotheby's and Christie's, offer buyers the same terms of business and recourse if items are not as presented as they do for items bought in their offline salesrooms. The challenge for the buyer is determining what level of responsibility is being assumed by which selling platform.

Not all of the advantages from the online environment are in the criminals' hands. Online audit trails, the ease of researching works' provenance and rapid international communication with enforcement agencies across the globe are some of the benefits a digital revolution has introduced for those investigating art crime.

Attempts to monitor the sale of art online have been limited. The UK's Portable Antiquities Scheme, set up in 1997 and funded by the Department for Culture, Media and Sport, has monitored the online sales of antiquities in a bid to identify potential treasure being sold. However, this has proved a challenge, particularly in the practicalities of gaining enough evidence from an online photograph and description to proceed with enquiries. The head of the scheme, Michael Lewis, describes how:

> With fine art, generally the concern is whether someone is selling an item as something it is not. With archaeology, the main concern is whether or not the item has been recovered (excavated) illegally and understanding its findspot. Proactive and systematic monitoring of sales online is resource-heavy, and we are no longer able to do that ourselves. However, many people are now aware that we are interested [in knowing about finds from metal detecting] and let us know any concerns, which works well. We still have an agreement with eBay, where we can monitor the site for objects.[56]

Fully comprehending the impact that the Internet is having, or will have, on criminal activity in the art market could be a book in itself.

Nevertheless, even a brief look at the opportunities emerging for fakes and stolen property on online selling platforms demonstrates the illicit opportunities that rapid technological innovation can open up.

CONCLUSION

Past examples of criminal activity involving art (whether a specific case, a cluster of activity within a particular region or area of the market or around a technological development) are a crucial means by which to learn how to prevent, detect and take action against similar criminality in the future. To some extent, the art market, law enforcement and the international community are using history (including very recent history) to guide future action, the key example being efforts to protect cultural property within periods of conflict (albeit many would prefer this learning to have occurred at a faster pace).

The trick to learning from the past, however, is to note that the factors you are looking out for as signs that an environment or moment could promise opportunities for art crime (discussed here: conflict, emerging markets and technological revolutions) are themselves fluctuating. The race to learn the latest developments, using past experiences as a guide, is, then, part of the ongoing struggle between the art market, criminals and law enforcement. Ultimately, it is a question of who can learn to adapt the quickest.

Chapter 2

A CRIME OF CONSEQUENCE

Standing in front of a group of students in London's Victoria and Albert Museum to provide a tour of an exhibition on fakes and forgeries that the Art & Antiques Unit had co-organised,[1] a member of the public interrupted me to declare that I was 'wasting police time . . . your team should be out on the streets of London tackling real crime, not chasing after paintings'.

This was not an isolated response to the fact that the UK's New Scotland Yard has an Art & Antiques Unit. It is, however, a response that partly derives from a belief that crimes involving art do not leave behind victims. Or, rather, they are crimes in which the victims are perceived as wealthy, careless and thus of lesser concern to much of society. This train of thought tends to continue along the lines that if art crime is of a lesser concern to the broader public, then it should be a lesser priority (if a priority at all) to the authorities. This chapter argues that such thinking underestimates the impact of art crime on individual victims, the art market and broader society.

While much attention is given to the perpetrators of art crime, less is understood of its victims, and the effect of crimes involving art is not well documented or quantified. The US$6 billion a year figure attributed to the value of stolen art internationally has already been mentioned, alongside the concerns that there is little methodology offered to back up this number. Nevertheless, if we compare this $6 billion figure to the estimated value of the world's art market, €51 billion[2] (or $53.9 million[3]), we can draw a very sweeping conclusion that art crime would appear to be a sizeable problem (if not a problem poised to cripple the sector entirely).

Any attempt to represent victims statistically is thwarted by the lack of appropriate data collection. Neither the US nor the UK has a means to bring together victim data on art crime, and the fact that victims are often hesitant to report crimes means that any figures which do exist will, at best, only be a partial representation of the true picture. A 1992 study by the academic Truc-Nhu Thi Ho, surveying dealers in New York, found that 14 of the 34 incidents of theft that occurred among the group had not been reported to police.[4] Survey participants gave explanations as to why they had not reported crimes, many of which could be reasons used regardless of the property involved: that is, a belief that police would not be able to do anything about the crime, that the loss was below the price needed to be insurance deductible, uncertainty that the property had not just been misplaced and wariness of confronting a suspect employee.

Missing from this list, but apparent in numerous criminal cases in the art market, is the fact that many professionals are ashamed or embarrassed to admit that an error has been made: be it mistakenly believing a fake art work to be genuine, or a security oversight. This is unsurprising for a sector in which reputation and specialist knowledge is critical for careers and where publicly funded cultural institutions have stakeholders to answer to and exist under the close scrutiny of the media.

This chapter considers the impact that crimes involving art can have on individual victims (e.g. the victim of a theft or forgery), the art market and broader society (i.e. not linked to the 'art world'). It also looks at the impact on those who are set to reap the benefits: that is, the perpetrators. For each grouping, even if there were firm data on the financial impact of art crime, there is also a need to acknowledge the historical, emotional, political and social consequences.

Today, there is widespread appreciation that cultural property equates to more than the sum of its parts, with cultural items possessing value well above the monetary. One of the most damaging consequences of crimes involving culture is the loss of history which disappears with objects (e.g. removing an antiquity without recording the original context in which it was found, or the confusion forgeries can introduce to art history). Likewise, there is increasingly widespread acknowledgement of the role that the destruction of cultural heritage can play in broader attacks on social identities and collective memories (see Chapter 1). Nevertheless, the emotional and reputational consequences of these crimes tend to be less considered or, at least, less prioritised in general coverage of the topic.

A need to demonstrate a crime's impact is not specific to the art world: police forces use impact statements across a range of crimes and jurisdictions, to demonstrate to courts the severity and broader implications of a crime. The government-run heritage protection and advice agency Historic England has published guidance on the use of impact statements within criminal cases involving heritage, arguing:

> [they] have proved invaluable in explaining the impact of crime on heritage assets both to the enforcing agency and also to the courts when considering a sentence. This has resulted in appropriate levels of sentencing that properly reflect the harm caused to the asset by the crime.[5]

Demonstrating that the impact of art crime is deeper and broader than typically understood, helps explain why there are demands for greater action to tackle the problem. It can also challenge belief that it is in the art market's interest to allow criminality to proliferate.

IMPACT ON INDIVIDUALS

There is such a depth of information about art restitution cases it can be easy to get lost in the lawsuits, ethical complexities and opinions. It is even easier to forget that there are individuals behind the headlines.

Melanie McFadyean is the granddaughter of Herbert M. Gutmann, a former director and son of the founder of Germany's Dresdner Bank. Having retired, Gutmann maintained a prominent role at the bank until 1933, when the influence of the Nazi party was strengthening. He soon found himself the subject of anti-Semitism and lost memberships of boards on which he had sat, facing mounting debts (primarily from the bank itself) and selling off parts of his art collection in an attempt to tackle them. In 1936, as the persecution of the Jewish people escalated, he fled to the UK. His brother and sister-in-law did not escape their home in the Netherlands and were subsequently killed.

Years later, in the 1980s, McFadyean's mother walked into the Courtauld Institute Galleries, in London, and recognised an oil sketch, *The Coronation of the Virgin*, *c.*1613, by Sir Peter Paul Rubens, which had once hung in her family home in Potsdam. When I asked Melanie McFadyean how she felt about the family's subsequent attempt at restitution of this picture, she answered: 'Bleak.' Two days later she wrote to me:

> I think bleak is a way of blocking out the welter of emotion that the second generation feels afraid of, maybe without realising it. I'm sure I'm not alone in this, under the ice of bleak is a meltdown of great hopeless sadness for what our families suffered, guilt that somehow you haven't felt bad enough about it at some stages in your life, overwhelmed by the task of trying to get anything back, confused by the financial gain that might come from it – why should you benefit from their loss? It doesn't bring them back or give anything to them. I think in the end what I wanted, as we tried to get the Rubens back, was to feel we had done right by my grandfather because I felt sure he had been forced to sell his art collection which included the Rubens and would never have done so if it hadn't been for the political situation in Nazi Germany.[6]

Many agreed with the family that Herbert M. Gutmann had been forced to sell, or surrender, his belongings. Another painting sold in the same auction as the Rubens, *Pappenheim's Death* by Hans Makart, was returned to the family by the Vienna Restitution Committee, in 2009, followed by the return of a painting by Franz von Lenbach, restituted by the German government in 2010. The family's former home in Potsdam was also restituted in the 1990s.

The UK Spoliation Advisory Panel, however, concluded that the sale of the Rubens had not been a 'forced' one. It judged that it is likely that Gutmann would have sold the work 'irrespective of any Nazi persecution' (although it did agree that anti-Semitism was the reason for Gutmann's loss of some supervisory roles in the bank).[7]

One of the daily and grim realities that gets overlooked in the shadows of academic and legal dissections of restitution cases or the excitement of high-value heists in the media, is the very real emotions for those embroiled in these cases. While a huge amount of literature has been devoted to the complex feelings which drive people to collect and keep art work,[8] the flipside of this desire to possess culture (i.e. when these items are lost, damaged or discovered to be something other than what was originally believed) is less considered.

Part of this tendency to overlook the personal loss of victims involved in art crime (or those embroiled in its ramifications later down the line, such as with some restitution cases or civil lawsuits) derives from the belief that those wealthy enough to own or trade in highly valuable art work (particularly contemporary art, the high prices for which still mystify many) are unlikely to feel any substantial financial destabilisation from its loss. As one art consultant recently complained to me, 'Fundamentally, people still think it's funny to laugh at rich people losing out.'

In reality, the range of victims caught up in art crime is as broad, deep and diverse as the market itself. It is also due to an increasing association in the public mind between the 'art world' and high-net-worth (and ultra-high-net-worth) sectors of society. Jan De Maere, the former president of the international art and antiques dealer association, CINOA, describes how:

> News headlines and front-page articles do not reflect the reality that art and antique dealers today account for 50 percent of global art world sales. This important group of dealers consists largely of discreet, low-profile individuals and small businesses

preferring to focus on finding great art to match with the right client rather than publishing high-flying sales prices.[9]

The impact of an art-related crime on victims is also not solely financial or directly proportionate to the amount of wealth stored in their bank accounts. The UK art dealer who owned the 14 art works (with a total estimated value of £1.7 million and including two paintings by Lowry) which were targeted as part of a raid on his home in 2007, where his wife and two-year-old daughter were threatened with a knife,[10] is likely to have suffered the same emotional impact as any other victim of an aggressive robbery. The emotional loss may indeed be higher, due to the emotional peculiarities of cultural property.

If a focus on high wealth skews understanding of the impact of art crime on some victims, understanding of how the vulnerable are affected by art crime deserves greater attention. Distracted burglaries, where criminals use deception to enter a property and later steal items, have long targeted art, antiques and war medals in the possession of the elderly. The term 'Brighton Knockers' was used to describe those in the UK town duping the elderly into selling their art and antiques for a far lower price than their actual worth or promising to 'restore' items before taking off with them for good. The strategy continues today. Sussex-based Lee Collins was convicted in 2010 for conning an elderly female and taking her jewellery, and was referenced in a warning issued by the Metropolitan Police Service about a broader scam involving leaflets being issued in the London borough of Westminster offering free valuations for antiques that were believed to be a 'cover for theft'.[11]

Artists (while not always the direct victim) are also impacted. When former art student Jonathan Rayfern admitted to the forgery of Tracey Emin's art works in 2010, the British artist reported feeling 'upset and distressed'.[12] Likewise, when Helaine Blumenfeld's 2-metre (7-foot) bronze sculpture *Transformation: Tree of Life* was recovered after being stolen from an art shipper, she claimed that 'This piece was a labour of love for me and I was devastated when it disappeared in 2005.'[13]

An understanding of the victims of art crime should also take into account the individual's treatment within the criminal justice system. This includes the likelihood of their being taken seriously, possible compensation, the loss of property and what happens to property seized during a criminal investigation. If there is a widespread perception that the authorities will not prioritise art crime cases (as appears to be the case), this may take us some way to understanding what is reported to law enforcement agencies and the decision of many victims to pursue alternative resolutions or civil law suits.

Unsurprisingly, there is little systematic data or research into the treatment of victims of art crime by law enforcement and the justice system. While certain professional groupings within the art sector, for example museums, will have direct channels of communication with law enforcement and can expect a fairly consistent response, the treatment of individual victims is more varied.

Individuals can find the criminal justice process for art crime a struggle, in terms of getting a police force to pursue a case. Providing the evidence needed can be the first hurdle. For every victim who sends the police comprehensive dimensions, condition notes and provenance history for a stolen painting, there is another victim who sends in a family photo of Aunt Betty wearing the stolen earrings in question – the only evidence that they have of ownership, and not a lot of help to a police investigation.

It is not unusual in large-scale art crime investigations, particularly those concerned with faked items, for a large number of witness statements and property to be collated. Only a proportion of the information and evidence seized is likely to be utilised within any subsequent trial. In the investigation into the prolific German art forger Wolfgang Beltracchi, only 12 of the 58 fakes identified by police were reportedly used as evidence in his 2011 trial and conviction.[14] This can leave a trail of unresolved issues, with owners left with art work that evidently came from the same source as works which were deemed stolen or fake and with no clear decision made as to the provenance or authenticity of the pieces in their possession. 'I'm in limbo,'[15] lamented one collector who had bought works said to be by the late Indian artist Francis Newton Souza on eBay, which he subsequently feared were fake after reading about the conviction of the British art forger William Mumford, who specialised in Indian Progressive art.

The decision as to what happens to art seized by police during the course of an investigation (regardless of whether it was used in a subsequent trial) tends to be made locally and has typically been left to the discretion of police and courtrooms. In some jurisdictions, judges have directed the destruction of works. In 2009, the owner of a drawing purportedly by Joan Miró was unable to prevent its destruction, after the work was deemed fake by a French auction house in 2013.[16] Conversely, a number of UK cases have seen judges allow items to be kept in police storage and used for 'educational purposes'.

Following a criminal case involving art, further victims may come forward, for example individuals who fear that works they own are similar to forgeries featured in a trial, or else those who recognise similarities in the circumstances in which a stolen or looted item was sold. Victims can seek to regain property or pursue damages via civil proceedings. The recent criminal investigation into Glafira Rosales' forgery of more than 60 fake modern artworks, to which she pleaded guilty in 2013, prompted a string of civil lawsuits, including that brought by the art collector Pierre Lagrange against the New York-based Knoedler Gallery over his 2007 purchase of a painting purportedly by Jackson Pollock.[17]

Nevertheless, financial compensation for victims is not guaranteed. The UK's Proceeds of Crime Act 2002 enables the civil recovery of proceeds of crime, and in the US there are mechanisms for restitution which victims can apply for, but the process is often lengthy or the assets in question are simply never found. The government may also choose to use the seized assets to cover its own costs, as well as seek to compensate victims – a famous Hawaiian case in 1993 resulted in a court's decision to sell on more than 12,000 unauthorised 'Salvador Dalí' prints and sculptures, in a bid to recoup the costs of the investigation.[18]

IMPACT ON THE ART MARKET

If the art market's practices and norms are seen directly or indirectly to facilitate criminal behaviour, it is unsurprising that the sector itself is rarely viewed as the main victim of illicit activity. However, despite claims that criminal behaviour is 'in the interest'[19] of individual professionals, businesses and the sector as a whole, at all levels it simply does not make business sense to support crime.

So what is the impact of crime on the art market? For individual professionals and art dealers in the sector, being a victim or perpetrator of crime can be ruinous. Naturally, being convicted for a crime is not a great advertisement for business. The New York art dealer Lawrence Salander, convicted in 2010 after pleading guilty to stealing $120 million from his clients, reportedly exclaimed: 'I've lost my wife, my business and my reputation.'[20]

Allegations of wrongdoing without a criminal conviction can be just as damaging within the close-knit network of the art trade. Witness the fall from grace of the UK-based furniture dealer John Hobbs, who was suspended from the British Antique Dealers' Association and faced financial struggles after a public claim that the works he was selling were heavily altered.[21] Conversely, the involvement of the Barakat Gallery in a very public battle with Iran over antiquities the latter claimed were illegally exported (although the legal proceedings were civil, rather than criminal) from its land between 2000 and 2004,[22] has done little to slow down the 100-year-plus business which continues to expand.

When art dealers fall victim to criminal activity (rather than being its perpetrators), the impact can also hit hard. While the media likes to concentrate on the blue-chip art dealers charging substantial fees in the glossy fairs of Miami and Basel, a 2010 survey by the arts research and consulting firm Arts Economics, looking at the market in its broader form, revealed that 'only 4% of dealers reported sales greater than €10 million each year'.[23] For such dealers, the loss of an art work or the realisation that a prized item is, in fact, a fake can have major consequences for the bottom line. Art lawyer Elizabeth Kessenides has also considered the tax implications arising from financial losses derived from art crime, in which the taxpayer must demonstrate a theft or 'prove that the seller defrauded him by knowingly and intentionally misattributing the painting to the artist'.[24]

A dealer's expertise in a subject matter can also be called into question when a work is wrongly authenticated or doubt is cast on its provenance. Professionals offering opinions on works of art, namely consultants and art historians (who are not typically discussed as part of the art market, but nevertheless play a crucial role within its mechanics), have also found their expertise under attack and, at worst, become involved in lawsuits (see Chapter 4, for a consideration of authentication panels).

Larger businesses in the art trade, such as auction houses, are also impacted by art crime. As Martin Wilson, Global Managing Director and General Counsel at Christie's for the geographical area from Europe to Asia, has commented: 'The reason we devote the resources and care to this issue [art crime] is that we know we are not judged on the 99 per cent of lots which sold without a problem; but on the 1 per cent that didn't.'[25] When crime is detected on their doorstep, their reputation can be irreversibly knocked. The obvious example is the 2002 price-fixing scandal between Sotheby's and Christie's, which resulted in a £13 million fine for the former and, in the US, a further £5.4 million fine and the imprisonment of Sotheby's former chairman, Alfred Taubman. Official punishments aside, the scandal further resulted in international media scrutiny – hardly the ideal scenario for Sotheby's, a business that prioritises its global reputation so greatly that it has press officers in more than 15 countries. Earlier allegations of Sotheby's involvement in the sale of looted antiquities was followed by the closure of the auction house's regular antiquities sales in London. While the company stated that it was a 'management decision',[26] rather than being linked to the allegations, it was a costly move considering Christie's brought in £21.1 million from its sales auction in that area in 2014 alone.[27]

The most reliable method of assessing the impact of crime on the art market is through the consideration of individual works of art or collections involved in criminal cases or embroiled in disputes. One of the most famous cases of this was the Sevso Treasure, a collection of fourth-century Roman artefacts which became the centre of a long-running ownership dispute between Lebanon, Croatia, Yugoslavia and Hungary following its emergence on the New York art scene in 1990. After the nations battled, but failed to prove their good title, the owner – the Marquess of Northampton – was found by the US court to be rightfully in possession of the artefacts.[28] However, despite the collection being worth an estimated £100 million on paper, the Marquess found it to be essentially unsaleable on the art market, where potential buyers were scared away by the apparent legal implications of getting involved (eventually, in 2014, a number of items were repatriated to Hungary, for a price). Similarly, in 2007, the Bulgarian government attempted to stop the London-based sale of a twelfth-century silver dish which it claimed was stolen: the sale went ahead nevertheless, but the dish failed to find a buyer.[29]

When criminal activity moves beyond a single work to the entire oeuvre of an artist or school of artists, the impact on that part of the market can be more far-reaching and long lasting. The markets for works by artists Amedeo Modigliani, Salvador Dalí, Andy Warhol and Jean-Baptiste-Camille Corot are known to be have suffered because of forgeries; indeed, it is anecdotally said in France that 'Corot painted 2,000 canvases, 5,000 of which are in America'.[30] In sectors of the art market where problems are repeatedly encountered, for example the emergence of illicitly removed objects in the antiquities sector, the market value of provenance is more pronounced. Two similar objects can differ stratospherically in price where an item with a foolproof ownership history dating back prior to 1970 (when the UNESCO Convention was drawn up) is up for sale next to an item with less information to hand. As one auction house employee anonymously put it to me, 'No one wants to buy themselves a future headache.'

There have been claims that art crime can boost the value of works of art. The scholar Jarrett Coomber argues that subsequent media attention following an art theft 'is, in a way, free marketing for the artist and their works' and uses statistical analyses to determine a 'five year "theft effect" whereby compound annual returns and auction sales for the selected artist were higher than in the five years prior to the theft'.[31] There is also some level of market value for fakes and forged works created by criminals involved in high-profile cases, including Elmyr de Hory whose fake Modigliani piece sold at Bonhams for £3,200,[32] and the 1990s British forger John Myatt, who has gone on to make a career out of 'copies' and by establishing a media presence. Nevertheless, this value remains a fraction of what the original works would have made, and the fame required to generate this level of interest is not gained by the majority of criminals working within the art market

What emerges from a consideration of the repercussions of art crime on the art market is the importance of reputation: to individual professionals, artists, businesses or the works of art themselves. The tight-knit nature of the art market which helps keep secrets under wraps is the same tight-knit nature which can make crime unappealing. Is it worth damaging the reputation which is core to your business for a quick buck?

BROADER SOCIETY'S EXPERIENCE

If there is a feeling that police time should be spent on tackling 'real crime' rather than crime in and around the art world, it is worth considering what 'real crime' is perceived to be. From conversations held with the public while working for the police, it strikes me that 'real crime', or crime viewed as being of greater importance, is generally considered to be an act which has an impact on a higher number of people in society (than art crime), or is considered to be of a greater physical threat.

This book does not argue that art crime should be law enforcement's greatest priority. It is, however, hoped that discussion of art crime's impact on broader society (i.e. not an impact solely felt by the art world and the players within and around it) could better demonstrate why resources are committed to the issue and why many are arguing for still more.

One of the oldest arguments as to why everyone is impacted by art crime is that culture forms part of a universal history that we all share. The looting of unrecorded antiquities is the obvious example, where the context of items may have had information to reveal and a potential contribution to our historical understanding of society's development. A 2000 report by the McDonald Institute for Archaeological Research further argued that: 'It is also possible to extract information about past climates and environments from properly contextualised paleontological and archaeological specimens, which have become a valuable resource as concerns grow over global warming and increasing levels of pollution.'[33] Additionally, the integrity of the object's appearance can be damaged by the rough way in which it has been removed, ranging from chisel marks to the commonly seen missing limb of sculptures.

The argument that cultural property is of universal importance, and thus crimes against or using it are of universal interest, has proven less accepted when it comes to fine art. Governments attempting to keep works of cultural significance within their borders and to repatriate works which they feel should be in their country (but are elsewhere) are adept at summarising the social and historical value of works of art. However, if a painting by a contemporary artist is stolen or missing, mainstream attention will primarily fall on the work's monetary value, rather than its importance to social history (unlike the loss of ancient art).

Holocaust restitution cases and examples of cultural property being targeted within conflict are broadening awareness of the deeper value of culture to societies, aside from monetary or historical value – i.e. in the construction of social identity and collective memory. Nevertheless, greater efforts could be made to communicate the human stories behind art works that are lost, simply because they can draw attention to the history that is being lost. When researching missing works from the UK's Government Art Collection in 2011, I discovered that a number of paintings created by artists on the Second World War frontlines, for the nation, had disappeared. One of these – *A Spotter, Heavy AA* (1942) by the Australian-born British painter Henry Lamb – had been on loan to the Ministry of Defence's school of Warminster in Wiltshire, before going missing between 1968 and 1980. Archives at the Imperial War Museum hold letters by the artist, written on the front line and describing the now-lost work. Reading and learning of the determination which went into creating the painting was moving: the letters may not raise the painting's monetary value, but they do act as a poignant reminder that the painting is a piece of a shared past, not just a canvas.

Less prominent in debates over losses to history through art crime, but as significant in terms of scale, are forgeries. Undetected fake objects and falsified provenances can corrupt understanding of individual artists and the society in which they lived, and can muddy the waters when attempting to make judgements on other works of art by the artist.[34]

Art-related criminal activity tends to be treated more seriously by a larger proportion of the public, when it is linked to other forms of criminality. The majority of criminals utilising or targeting art in criminal activity do not specialise in this area alone. While art forgery tends to be more specialised (because of the resources/specialist knowledge required), opportunistic burglars grabbing antique silverware, armed robbers who have spent months planning a museum raid and looters targeting tombs are all 'art criminals' who typically possess a CV with previous experience in a range of offences.

Where cultural property is used within a broader scheme of criminal activity, the impact of art crime on broader society is easier to communicate. The unravelling of drug trafficking, money laundering and tax evasion schemes have demonstrated the position of culture at the heart of seemingly unrelated criminal activity. Examples include the 2005 discovery of a painting by Picasso, *Nature Morte à la Charlotte* (1924), stolen from the Centre Pompidou in Paris and reportedly found by police searching a drug trafficker's residence.[35] Further, while art can be discovered when looking for drug networks, the opposite scenario is equally true: the identification of a stolen painting can be a very resource-friendly way for the police to begin gathering the evidence to identify a criminal network.

The manifold impacts of art crime on society should not underplay the value of the sector itself or suggest it requires this justification to be considered a concern. Indeed, the fact that the UK art market supported more than 7,850 businesses and paid around £1.6 billion in tax in 2013,[36] and that the world's art market is estimated to be worth €51 billion,[37] demonstrates a sizeable sector within society, which deserves as much attention as any.

THE PERPETRATOR'S EXPERIENCE

One of the more interesting questions to ask an art forger is how he or she felt at the moment of being caught. In my experience, the answer often includes the word 'relief'. While much effort has been devoted to understanding the motives of criminals working with or around cultural property, which are typically financial (as this book has also suggested – see Introduction), a focus on motive alone does oversimplify the process that the criminal has often gone through.

When the convicted UK art forger John Myatt spoke of his descent into creating art forgeries, he described a process of having started doing copies, trying a few fakes and then spiralling into a mini production line. This is not unusual. One forger, released from a sentence but wishing to remain anonymous, told me of how he had started: 'I used to "embellish" pre-existing paintings to attract tourists – add things like hot-air balloons in the corner, a flag or something. Then I was painting eighteenth-century art. There was no lying involved. I wasn't very good.' After the arrival of children and responsibilities, things became more deliberate: 'Things just spiralled. I was never a copyist. But I began to paint the one that got away.'[38]

Unsurprisingly, the wide range of criminals targeting or using cultural property prevents any sweeping statements about how the criminality impacts their lives. However, it is worth considering the impact of the offences when it goes smoothly for the criminals – that is, when they do not get caught. While there is indisputably a large amount of wealth in the art market, many art crimes (primarily theft and forgery, rather than crimes using art to disguise larger profits, such as in money laundering) generate a relatively modest profit. Reports that stolen art will only attract 7 to 10 per cent of its true value on the black market[39] sound logical, given that the majority of lower-end crimes will see burglars selling paintings quickly for a fast profit and that the higher-end items are too risky to sell at market value. Profits are highly variable in the illicit antiquities trade also, with estimates suggesting that 98 per cent of profit will go to the 'middleman' or the individual(s) fencing the property into the legitimate trade and the original finder receiving a relative pittance.[40] Similarly, I have yet to meet an art forger who is living in luxury.

The impact on criminals is clearly more profound when things go wrong – that is, when they get caught. While relief may be an initial feeling for many art forgers, this is more insightful of the process leading them into the crime (as mentioned, often described as 'spiralling') than a reflection of their thoughts on what will happen post-arrest.

The justice system's treatment of crimes involving cultural property can vary greatly in its severity, depending on the price point and significance of property involved, geography, politics and even the judge on the day. There are signs that the US at least is becoming more punitive in its treatment of art crimes. The US Sentencing Commission (USSC) introduced some tougher penalties for the theft of cultural property in 2002, and 'determined that a separate guideline [for sentencing for crimes involving cultural heritage] is needed that specifically recognizes both the federal government's longstanding obligation and unique role in preserving these resources and the harm caused to the nation and its inhabitants when its history is degraded through the destruction of cultural heritage resources.'[41] Nevertheless, many argue that punishments need to be more consistent and substantial (see Chapter 6).

Once a criminal sentence has been completed and an art criminal is released, there appear to be multiple career routes available. Some are known to reoffend, including the UK-based Gary Doyle, who was convicted for the 2011 theft of six maps from Forty Hall Museum in north London.[42] A year later, he was released and wanted by police again for an alleged theft from a cultural institution. A subsequent 'chance encounter' with a security manager from the Victoria and Albert Museum led to his being arrested again and later sentenced to two years in prison.[43]

For art forgers, the career options seem broader following release, as the media is happy to bestow a degree of respect on such crimes, offering interviews and even TV series.

Less is known about the degree to which criminals involved with art understand the impact which their crimes have. It can be presumed, in keeping with the general public's opinion, that the majority of criminals targeting art perceive it to have an impact on a fairly narrow and wealthy portion of society (unless, say, they are criminals knowingly targeting the vulnerable and elderly for antiques in burglaries, rather than those aiming to catch out an unsuspecting investor with fake and pricey contemporary art). It is possible here to draw a comparison with those who steal from larger corporations, with the mind-set that a larger company can better absorb the losses.

The anonymous forger discussed at the start of this section was shocked to learn that this was not always the case and that an elderly couple had lost a sizeable chunk of their pension from his deception. Similarly, an account of the British forger Eric Hebborn by the journalists Laney Salisbury and Aly Sujo echoes this sense that art crime would only have the potential to impact those who would not greatly feel it:

He refused – or failed – to see the criminality 'in making a drawing in any style one wishes . . . and asking an expert what he thinks of it,' Hebborn wrote in his autobiography *Drawn to Trouble: Confessions of a Master Forger*. He claimed to be a fair player in this game of wits because he was levelling the playing field. He established his own moral guideline of sorts: One of his rules was that he would never sell a work to someone who was not a recognised expert or acting on expert advice.[44]

CONCLUSION

Part of the hurdle in demonstrating the wide reaching impact of these crimes is the difficulty of articulating the value of property beyond a price tag and that the consequences of this sort of crime run deeper than pockets alone. Another part derives from misconceptions that only a small, wealthy portion of society is affected. Arguments that the sector is content directly, or indirectly, to allow such criminal activity are further challenged by the fact that the art market itself consistently stands to be the biggest loser from it.

Chapter 3

WHEN IS A PROBLEM A PROBLEM?

As I stood in Sotheby's in London in 2011, an announcement rang out; 'Lot 73, *Albert Bridge*, 1952, by William Brooker, has been removed from sale.'[1] There was little reaction in the room to this news, aside from the sound of my scrabbling through the sale catalogue. There it was. In all its glossy-paged glory, the painting I had seen listed as 'missing' on the UK Government Art Collection's online database.

If the painting did not make it to the saleroom, it had certainly been on display the week before in the pre-auction exhibition. A label described the painting's history as 'Leicester Galleries, 1952'. The catalogue added that any further details about the work's past 'were untraced'. This did not necessarily mean untraceable. Having viewed the work to confirm it was the missing painting, I spoke to one of the sleekly clad sales representatives. She knew very little about the painting's history but told me that, 'You could always try to find out more, if you're that interested.'

I was interested. But as the painting was quietly withdrawn from sale it struck me that very few others were. There were no awkward questions asked in the subsequent coverage of the auction and no public explanation as to how the painting had gone missing from the British Embassy in Gibraltar, at some point, and ended up in a London saleroom years later.[2]

The lack of general interest in the work's reappearance has stayed with me. It is natural that a work of a moderate price (the pre-sale estimate was pitched under £10,000) should attract less media attention than the headline-grabbing million-dollar sales, but as a painting lost within a government building, I had expected greater furore.

So, what is it that makes us care about one case involving art (whether criminal, civil or simply unexplained) more than another? It would appear to be a cocktail of public pressure, media coverage, political agendas and law enforcement resources. Determining the measures and components of this cocktail is crucial in understanding why one case can sit unconsidered for years, while others go straight to the top of a police officer's pile. Take, for example, the UK politician, Boris Johnson, who in 2004 announced in the House of Commons that he had 'a slightly guilty conscience' as he had 'liberated' a cigar case belonging to, and found in the house of, the former Iraqi Foreign Minister Tariq Aziz a few days after the war.[3] While a cigar case may appear to be a relatively minor issue in comparison to other items of cultural property, in terms of scale and importance, the piece was considered of 'cultural importance' by the Iraqi Embassy. The case was investigated and the item returned at a rapid speed, an urgency one would not expect if the case had been played out more privately and with fewer political parties involved.

The same cocktail of factors that influence responses to individual cases can help us understand how art crime is dealt with by society in general. It is easy to say that there are insufficient resources allocated to tackling the problem. However, until one figures out how the problem is understood by those allocating the resources, the push for more will struggle to succeed.

This chapter considers how, why and when different and overlapping sectors of society consider art crime to be a problem (namely, academia, the media, the art market and the authorities). This should help us better understand society's responses to the subject and which sectors of society are instrumental in instigating action against art crime.

A common concern amongst all these groups when considering or articulating the importance of a particular art crime – or the issue in general – is the value of the cultural property in question. Whether a journalist working on a news desk, an academic attending a conference or a politician entering a briefing, the value (whether monetary, historical or social) of the cultural property in question tops the list when arguing for action. A common point of difference is whose responsibility it is to protect this value.

A PROBLEM . . . WHEN LAW ENFORCEMENT SAYS SO?

As the saying goes, *nullum crimen sine lege*: no crime without law. If there can be no 'crime' without laws in place to designate certain acts as 'criminal', there can be no enforcement of these laws without the political will and resources in place to drive enforcement. Considering how a known area of crime in the art market shifts to becoming an issue which 'needs to be dealt with' in the eyes of many, and in the eyes of those in the position to deal with the criminality, is not an academic exercise alone. A sizeable proportion of time and resources within the Art & Antiques Unit can be spent justifying both the team and individual cases it is dealing with – to its superiors, the public and prosecution services.

It is interesting to note the responses of law enforcement agencies to art crime. The UK's *Independent* newspaper claimed in 1996 that: 'Interpol, and the police forces of its 177 member countries, treat [art theft] as a tiresome irrelevance, going through the motions of tackling it without any expectations of success.'[4] Nicholas Brett, the Underwriting Director from AXA Art Insurance, suggests that the rapidity and strength of police response appears to be based on the type of offence, rather than the value or specifics of an object: 'If someone is hurt or threatened, or there appear links to organised crime, then law enforcement is clearly more interested [in an art crime case].'[5]

Specialist police units for art crime were not set up in the UK and US until 1969 and 2004 respectively. The development of dedicated resources to the sector can be linked to specific moments of heightened crime. The author and professor Laurie Adams describes the formation of the UK's Art & Antiques Unit in 1969 at a time in which there was 'an explosion of interest in antiques' whereby '£100,000 worth of antiques and £30,000 to £40,000 worth of paintings and sculptures'[6] were being stolen in London every month. A now-closed art police unit existed in Sussex, England, due to the high level of art and antiquities stolen from across the nation later turning up in the town's stalls and stores. In the US, the formation of a specialist federal squad occurred partly as a response to the 2003 ransacking of the Baghdad Museum in Iraq, and surrounding international pressure on market countries to tighten regulation.

In 'source' countries, or those where the supply of cultural property within the country outweighs domestic demand (and is at risk of being removed to cater for demand elsewhere), specialist art crime teams tend to be larger. For example, Italy has a dedicated team of around three hundred officers. In 'market' countries, where demand for cultural property outweighs supply, resources are smaller; the US currently has a rapid deployment art crime team of 16 officers,[7] who deal with relevant cases where they emerge in the officer's allocated region, but not a full-time department solely focused on the issue. In the UK, a specialist team is maintained but kept small in numbers: currently there are four officers. Discussions of expanding units have occurred, the UK's House of Commons debate in 2007 being an example, but it was argued that 'it is obviously for the commissioner to determine operational priorities, and he believes that he has it about right'.[8]

The UK's Association of Chief Police Officers announced a Heritage and Cultural Property Crime Working Group in 2013, which consolidated a network of around 20 local authorities, alongside representatives of the Department for Culture, Media and Sport, the National Crime Agency, English Heritage and the Metropolitan Police Service, with a goal of 'providing an overview of the key issues affecting the prevention, enforcement and sharing of intelligence in relation to crimes and anti-social behaviour committed against heritage assets and cultural property in the United Kingdom.[9] A key reason used to not expand specialist resources on a full-time basis is that the core team would receive broader support from its police force when required. In the UK, other specialist units (for example the Money Laundering team which is also based within the Specialist & Economic Crime Directorate) would support the work of the Art & Antiques Unit with resources for operations or with intelligence. Moreover, not all criminal activity that could be considered 'art crime' is dealt with by dedicated Art units. Local police forces will typically be the first on hand to report art theft and fraud cases, with support or investigation from a specialist team only being provided when the additional expertise is felt to be necessary.[10] Police forces in both the UK and US were dealing with art crimes long before they established specific teams for the problem.

Enforcement agencies at customs also play a crucial role through preventing and investigating the illegal export of cultural property, looted items and stolen works of art (which is a far easier way to transport assets across borders than cash). For example, the US has a distinct Cultural Property, Art and Antiquities Investigations (CPAA) team, established within the customs department.[11] One of the most important discoveries of stolen art in recent years, that of Cornelius Gurlitt's stash of more than 1,200 works of art seized by the Nazis and collated by his art dealer father, was sparked by a custom official's search in 2014.[12] Meanwhile, 'Operation Mummy's Curse', run by US immigration and Customs Enforcement, has reportedly resulted in the seizure of more than $2.5 million worth of stolen antiquities.[13]

Although this broader range of resources available for tackling art crime is more promising than the initial assessment of a small team of art detectives working alone, it can also lead to an inconsistent approach to art crime across the country. Any attempt to understand whether police are interested in art crime has to acknowledge that responses across different police forces in the same country will vary widely, but it is worth getting to know how the issue is perceived by them.

Inconsistency in how criminal offences are recorded can be as varied from force to force, as how they are investigated. To demonstrate this diversity, I attempted to collate figures for UK crimes involving art and antiques within a specific year, by contacting 45 police forces across English, Scotland, Wales and Northern Ireland with the same request for data on art crimes between 2014 and 2015.[14] It only took three responses to realise just how unlikely a useable set of data on art crime statistics from UK police forces could be.

The key issue with drawing together sets of comparable data was that the systems used to record crimes have disparate ways of recording the type of property involved in a crime. While the majority of forces had broader categories of property which would then require manual searching to identify whether any details of 'art' or 'antiquities' had been noted. Not only did these differing categorisations prevent useable comparisons being made between forces' data, they also prevented a number of the requests for information from being fulfilled as it would take officers over the allotted research time (for a freedom of information request). Less than half of the forces could supply all or a proportion of the data requested, with more than a thousand crimes reported but little further useable detail available.

Data that was provided from forces also revealed the system's dependence on individual officers recording objects in sufficient detail to offer an accurate picture of items affected. There were also clear anomalies in the research, including a crime report from Northern Ireland which recorded a 'tube of paint' as an art or antique.

Police working at borough level deal with such a breadth of criminal offences and a diverse range of sectors that this inconsistency in defining what is 'art' or an 'antique' is not surprising. I recently spoke to a police officer from a regional UK police force about art crime and received the following response:

> My perception is that art crime is not treated as any more of a priority than any other crime. I'd say that the majority of officers wouldn't treat a stolen piece of art any differently to any other kind of stolen property. In my opinion the amount of research done to trace the item would depend on the officer. Also the nature of art might cause difficulties – some officers might struggle when told that an, apparently mundane, item (like a ball or a light bulb, for instance) could be worth tens of thousands of pounds and the seriousness of the crime might be lost. I know of a case where an officer had to determine the

> authenticity of an art work and he really had no idea where to start with this. I can't say that I would either, and we have no specific training in relation to crimes involving art.[15]

The inconsistency between the police data from the freedom of information requests and the police officer quoted here demonstrate that the strength of a specialist unit lies is in its ability to collate pan-regional intelligence and offer specialist advice. Intelligence includes the stolen art databases run by the Metropolitan Police Service and the FBI (see Chapter 6).

Evidential challenges faced in an art crime case demonstrate how, to some extent, art is necessarily treated in the same way as other types of property. This approach has been criticised. The criminologist John E. Conklin suggests:

> The paucity of law-enforcement resources devoted to the investigation of art crime reflects, in part, an attitude that art is just another kind of property, even if it has a high market value. That attitude minimises the uniqueness of artworks and their importance to a people's cultural heritage, factors that warrant the devotion of greater law-enforcement resources to the problem of art crime.[16]

Despite this apparent shortcoming on the part of law enforcement, this approach is necessary to meet the evidential requirements and priorities of the prosecution services (in the UK, the Crown Prosecution Service; in the US, via attorneys) and convince a jury, which may not possess specialist knowledge of the sector. Nevertheless, the 'uniqueness' of art, which Conklin is concerned with, while not always the focus of the investigation, can play a crucial role in expressing the impact a crime has had, an impact which prosecution services do take seriously (see discussion of impact statements in Chapter 2).

Law enforcement resources specifically devoted to art crime are lean. But these dedicated units are supported by a broader framework of intelligence and resources which will deal with any reported crime. This may still be deemed insufficient by many, but it is nonetheless a larger response than a sweeping count of art-devoted units would initially suggest.

A PROBLEM . . . WHEN ACADEMICS SAY SO?

Academia has remained fairly consistent in its view that art crime is a 'problem', and one that requires more attention from governments and the art market itself. Indeed, it is a pretty powerful body of opinion: providing the research and voice to influence government action, forming direct relationships with the media and, at times, providing the knowledge to sway the outcome of individual criminal cases (e.g. identifying a work as fake or having been dug up within a particular region).

Academic influence on the treatment or prioritisation of action against art crime has been most persistent and influential on the issue of the looting of antiquities. Coverage of the topic accelerated in the 1960s and 1970s.[17] Of the same period, Professor of Anthropology Karen D. Vitelli notes that 'the focus of archaeology moved from the wonderful and curious objects and monuments of earlier generations to broader questions about how and, more importantly, why people in the past had organised their lives as they did.'[18] This broader perspective naturally stimulated a desire to better understand the context in which items were discovered, in order to prevent this context from being lost in an illicit removal. The legal author Asif Efrat argues that the advocacy of American archaeologists subsequently played 'a key role in educating policymakers about the loss of historical knowledge caused by looting and the necessity of regulation'[19] in the lead up to the US's ratification of the 1970 UNESCO Convention on the Means of Prohibiting and Preventing the Illicit Import, Export and Transfer of Ownership of Cultural Property.

This influential role was furthered by archaeologists and heritage professionals in the UK, with the creation of the Illicit Antiquities

Research Centre at the University of Cambridge's McDonald Institute for Archaeological Research in 1996. This (now-closed) group published research, raised awareness on the issue of looted antiquities and directly called for UK government action. Today, the Scottish Centre for Crime and Justice Research works with a team of academics and scholars specialising in the subject and has collated background papers to support policy decisions, including a background paper for a 2009 meeting held in Vienna by the United Nations Office on Drugs and Crime.[20] Further organisations collating and commissioning relevant research include the Association for Research into Crimes against Art (ARCA), the Institute of Art and Law and the International Foundation for Art Research.

Influential academics leading calls for action include the UK-based Professor Norman Palmer, Dr Neil Brodie and Professor Colin Renfrew (Lord Renfrew of Kaimsthorn) while, in the US, Patty Gerstenblith, a research professor at Chicago's Center for Art, Museum & Cultural Heritage Law officially chairs a Cultural Property Advisory Committee. It should also be noted that despite a history of antagonism between the archaeologist and art trade communities, there have been numerous examples of their working together to push for action against illicit trade, including the UK's Ministerial Advisory Panel on Illicit Trade, which was both set up and produced its final report in the year 2000.

If academia can provide the facts and figures to prompt change, it can equally cause as much debate as it does resolution. A 2011 report by Tess Davis, the assistant director of the Cambodia-based, not-for-profit organisation Heritage Watch, outlined a correlation between the looting of Khmer artefacts and Sotheby's sales (between 1988 and 2010), subsequently arguing that 'This correlation suggests an illegal origin for much of the Khmer material put on the auction block by Sotheby's'.[21] Her argument was supported by her study of provenances included in auction house catalogues. Davis concluded that 71 per cent of objects had 'no published provenance or ownership history, meaning that they could not be traced to previous collections, exhibitions, sales or publications'. Further, she argued that 'fluctuations in the sale of the unprovenanced pieces can also be linked to events that would affect the number of looted antiquities exiting Cambodia and entering the United States'. Sotheby's response to the report was prompt, requesting Davis to retract the paper.[22] In its letter to the Davis, the auction house argued that the paper lacked 'credible factual support' and that the amount of provenance detail included in catalogues had increased over time. It argued that not publishing all such information about an item did not mean provenance had been unavailable or unexplored.

When it comes to offering opinions on the authenticity of an art work, academics and art experts can face criticism and even legal challenges – or, rather, accusations of being negligent or deliberately manipulative in the formation of those opinions (as with challenges against auction houses and authentication panels: see Chapter 4). Nevertheless, the value of expert opinions as witness statements within criminal cases involving art (from forgeries, to thefts, to illicitly removed items), and in offering guidance to the progression of police investigations, should not be underestimated; nor should the importance of academic freedom for the health of the art market.

If experts are increasingly wary to commit to opinions on specific artefacts or works of art, others are among the most vocal in society on the subject of art crime in general. Journalists looking for quotes, facts or images are often in touch with academics who are subsequently fairly powerful, in terms of informing public opinion on the subject.

Despite it often being said that academia has neglected the topic of art crime, it has in fact paved the way and led much discussion on the issue. Typically, this discussion is directly or indirectly critical of the art trade or advocates change within it.

A PROBLEM . . . WHEN THE MEDIA SAYS SO?

A journalist pitching an art crime story to a newspaper editor will likely hear some (or all) of the following questions: What art was involved? Was it valuable? Who was to blame?

These also tend to be the questions in the minds of much of the public (many of whom have had little former experience or awareness of art crime) when faced with news of an art crime. Newspaper coverage, documentaries, television coverage and fictional representations of the subject subsequently play a key role in informing and shaping opinions about the subject. Of course, not everyone adopts the same attitude as the media takes on, but that the media has an influence is clear: indeed, a 2013–14 report by the UK's Office for National Statistics found that 67 per cent of the public reported to have had their perceptions of crime informed by news and television programmes.[23]

Media interest in art crime had picked up a pace by the late 19th century. Newspaper reports regularly detailed art thefts and rewards up for offer, while the topic of art fraud was covered with a 'peer-to-peer' tone adopted to warn other collectors of frauds. A patronising tone when describing the plight of those caught out by crimes was equally evident from an early stage. An 1895 British newspaper article describes how:

> Formerly the average collector was a shrewd individual who, from his knowledge and experience, was able at once to distinguish between the genuine and the spurious. He did not collect merely because it was the fashion to do so, like many modern collectors . . . He therefore gave no encouragement to dishonest folk either in respect of ignorance, gullibility, or a yearning to be in the forefront of fashion.[24]

While news coverage of crimes involving art and the trade in cultural property is evident since the early phases of the art market, it was a number of powerful pieces of investigative journalism from the 1970s onwards that saw the media's role expanding from reportage to include an examination of the trade's practices. Notable examples include Karl E. Meyer's 1973 book *The Plundered Past*,[25] which identified links between the infrastructure of the market and illegal activity; investigative journalist Peter

Watson's 1998 *Sotheby's: The Inside Story*, which explored the auction house's sale of looted antiquities; and the same author's 2006 *The Medici Conspiracy* (written with researcher Cecilia Todeschini), which further followed the involvement of the antiquities dealer Giacomo Medici in his sale of numerous looted antiquities to high-profile US cultural organisations (including the J. Paul Getty Museum in Los Angeles and the Metropolitan Museum in New York).

Peter Watson's work, in particular, demonstrates the very real impact media coverage of the topic can have. Not only did the journalist's research expand police investigations into involved parties, but it also contributed to a situation today in which the practices of the art trade are no longer able to exist without a very real media and public scrutiny.

Much of this scrutiny continues to focus on the looting of antiquities. Today, coverage tends to be preoccupied with potential links between the illicit activity and broader criminal or terrorist networks. For example, a 2015 article in the *Guardian* newspaper followed Mark Altaweel, a Near East specialist from University College London's Institute of Archaeology, on a hunt to track down 'blood antiquities'.[26] While looting is increasingly reported with a grave tone and with recognition of the importance of cultural heritage, the continued press fascination with art forgery cases is far more light-hearted. The *Daily Mail*, for example, reported in 2007 on 'The artful codgers: Pensioners who conned British museums with £10m forgeries',[27] with very little sympathy for victims. Meanwhile the German newspaper *Der Spiegel* describes how the art forger Wolfgang Beltracchi is, in fact, admired by some:

> Finally, there are the enlightened art lovers who admired this hippie-like desperado, because he pulled the wool over the eyes of the art world and, in doing so, exposed a system in which millions are paid for paintings whose authenticity is very difficult to determine – a system that makes erratic decisions about which art is worth a lot and which is worth nothing at all, and that doesn't even seem to know exactly what art is.[28]

While an individual conducting credit-card fraud requires a certain skill to enact a crime, these skills are rarely depicted in the media in such a celebratory fashion.

The media's current relationship with the art market also reflects its broader interest in the levels of transparency in, and regulation of, high-wealth sectors (see Introduction). Media coverage of concerns over money-laundering and tax-evasion schemes involving art, for example, echo the terminology around concerns of the finance sector existing outside scrutiny. Directly comparing the art trade against other sectors is increasingly common. The *New York Times* reported the views of James R. Hedges IV, a New York collector and financier, who said in 2013: 'The art world feels like the private equity market of the '80s and the hedge funds of the '90s . . . It's got practically no oversight or regulation.'[29]

When it comes to reporting and examining art crime, media coverage is informative, amused and generally critical of the market in which the crimes function. This scrutiny is, of course, crucial to any sector's health within a democracy, and journalism in this field has played a key role in driving public and political opinion on the subject and pressure to make changes (e.g. the UK's joining of UNESCO). However, an impression within the trade that the media often takes a viewpoint of 'guilty until proven innocent' can also have a negative impact, with professionals working in the sector often feeling unable to talk about concerns openly and honestly.

A PROBLEM . . . WHEN THE ART MARKET SAYS SO?

A crucial step in tackling any problem is the acceptance that there is a problem in the first place. For many dealers, professionals and businesses in the sector there is a view that while criminal issues occasionally arise, it is not yet at a stage or scale where concentrated action is required.

Getting an accurate grip on how those in the industry feel about art crime is challenging, to say the least. There is widespread reluctance from individuals and organisations to talk about the issue. This does not mean, however, that the whole industry is in denial; nor does it demonstrate an inherent desire to support crime (although it is clear that some in the sector fit into these categories). The hesitance to talk openly about the issue can also be attributed to a reluctance to unnerve the market they function in and the clients they serve, and to a lack of confidence in discussing the topic. As discussed above, the media has a strong track record in mocking the market's shortcomings and leading accusations against its behaviour.

If spoken accounts about the scale and impact of criminal activity in the market are hard to attain from the market players themselves, observing their behaviour can prove more insightful that there is a problem they feel needs attention. Major auction houses are proactive in their approach to restitution cases, provenance research and anti-money-laundering measures. In 2000, Christie's decided that as a matter of policy they would not sell objects where there was no pre-2000 provenance. Then, as a tightening of that policy, the auction house required verifiable evidence of that pre-2000 provenance. A number of the founding stakeholders of the Art Loss Register were also from the art market (see Chapter 4). These measures are not always filtering down to smaller businesses, which are often run single-handedly and do not take extensive precautions as 'know-your-customer' background checks as a matter of course. This could be as much a symptom of having known their customers for years, as of a lack of concern over the risks of criminality.

Concrete changes have been attained with pressure from key market players, including the development of the Dealing in Cultural Objects (Offences) Act 2003 and the market's support of the 1994 abolishment of the UK's historical *marché ouvert* law (which allowed criminals to sell stolen goods between sunrise and sunset in nominated areas, without provenance and with title of ownership legally obtained). The previously mentioned 2000 Ministerial Advisory Panel on Illicit Trade included, alongside other key academics and archaeologists, Anthony

Browne (Chairman of the British Art Market Federation), James Ede (Director of the Antiquities Dealers Association) and Joanna van der Lande (an Associate Director of Bonhams). The art trade's prominent role in these discussions supports Anthony Browne's assertion that: 'When there has been a gap in existing legislation which can be filled by introducing new laws which target the criminal without enveloping the legitimate market in unnecessary red tape, we have always supported the required changes.'[30] Where patterns of criminal activity threaten the market's profit margins, efforts have also been made to tackle the problem. Obvious examples include measures taken and resources developed to detect forgeries. Catalogues raisonnées are considered by the market to be the definitive listing of a particular artist's work, while authentication panels are also a popular means by which market players can seek to demonstrate that work is as pertained.[31]

Despite the central role the art market plays within the subject of art crime, key representatives from the market – specifically, auction houses and trade associations) – are often less prominent in conferences and publications focused solely on the issue. Martin Wilson, told me: 'We [Christie's] ensure that we are present at conferences, such as UNESCO, or events covering current conflicts and government meetings on prevalent issues. Our time and resources are limited, however, and we focus most on those conferences and events which can help us make positive changes and assist in the tackling of these issues.'[32]

Regardless of whether measures taken to prevent and detect criminal activity are born of reputational, legal, moral or business motives – or whether the measures are deemed to go far enough – it is clear that the sector as a whole does take action where and when it feels it is required.

A PROBLEM . . . WHEN GOVERNMENTS SAY SO?

However impassioned a police officer may feel about a missing painting, however angrily an article in the press may condemn antiquities looting, however convincing a body of academic research into the scale of art fraud may be; unless political thought is running in the same direction, one can expect very little real change in the allocation of greater resources to tackling art crime. For some, including Noah Charney, a professor of art history specialising in art crime, governments are not taking art crime seriously enough:

> Most countries have no dedicated art police, an important point to note, as it is evidence that the governmental administration of these countries do not consider art crime of sufficient severity to warrant a department of their own, despite numerous publications to the contrary. The reason for this is the relative paucity of sufficiently extensive empirical data and statistics on art crime – the result of a cyclical self-destructive pattern. They do not dedicate resources because the existing data has not proven its extent and severity to them.[33]

Political action on issues involving cultural property has historically needed a bit of a prompt: be it a war to inspire sanctions on imports of antiquities, an embarrassing public scandal to open eyes on the former lack of provenance in the art trade, or some external pressure on the issue (e.g. from the archaeological community). Governments also recognise that the resolution of high-profile disputes involving works of art can act as a good-news story for the media, or as a diplomatic tool. The return of two statues, reportedly smuggled out of India in 2009 and returned by the US government, was described by one newspaper as 'a move to repair damaged political relations in the wake of a diplomatic spat'.[34] On the flipside, unresolved disputes can quickly attract awkward attention – the entrance of Amal Clooney, the human rights lawyer and wife of film actor George Clooney, into the ongoing ownership dispute over the Elgin Marbles between the Greek and UK governments being one very public example.

Many of the actions taken by governments on crimes involving art or cultural property are linked to a specific problem, for example looted antiquities being imported from Iraq or the need to close a loophole in pre-existing legislation. However, there are also signs that the protection of cultural property has made its way onto government agendas as a more permanent fixture. The US and UK's signing of numerous international conventions concerned with protecting cultural heritage (see Chapter 5) reflect a growing recognition that the importance of cultural property is more than a sum of its parts, including appreciation of the role it plays in identity-making and the collective memories of a society.

Where there is evidence that cultural property is being used as a means to fund the type of criminal activity which is topping governments' agenda, the plight of culture can also climb its way up the agenda. For example, links between terrorism and the looting of antiquities would certainly catch the eye of politicians more readily than pleas for support in reducing art fraud.

Despite this growing appreciation of cultural heritage, art crime per se is simply not a top priority for governments. This does not, however, mean that works of art, and the art market itself, are not impacted by actions governments take against the issues which do top their action lists. Works of art and the surrounding trade repeatedly feature in criminal investigations spurred by broader international measures taken against corruption, tax evasion, terrorism and money laundering. Recent such headlines include the 2015 seizure of a painting, possibly by Leonardo da Vinci, in Switzerland during an investigation into tax crime[35] and the French authorities' charging of art dealer Guy Wildenstein for tax evasion in 2013.[36] While these cases were not motivated by a desire to crack down on the art market per se, they offer evidence that the art market is not immune to broader crackdowns in society.

The reality is that challenging any government's commitment to preventing crime in the art market is unlikely to be as effective as demonstrating to governments how fighting crime involving art fits in with their broader priorities. This is not to admit that art crime is of lesser importance or does not deserve greater attention: it is merely acknowledgement that, in the short term, this would be a more efficient strategy to raise resources allocated to the sector.

CONCLUSION

When is a problem a problem? When those concerned about a particular case or the broader issue of criminal activity within the art market are those same people in a position to do something about it.

Understanding how law enforcement, academics, the media, the art market and governments understand crime involving art can lead to more useful conversations about how changes can be made to prevent them. The motivations and limitations of these groupings differ: media outlets, for example, need to sell papers; enforcement agencies are acting within the boundaries of a wider legal and political system; and the art market itself is concerned with its own financial health (obviously these are sweeping generalisations). There will always be limited success in convincing any of these groups that there should be a greater focus on tackling art crime, if the way in which they understand the problem and reasons for wanting action to be taken are not considered.

There is no 'correct' reason to care about art crime, or at least no reason which all will agree on. However, determining why someone does or does not care is probably the most effective way to go about working with them to agree on future ways of tackling it.

PART II

THE HEROES

Chapter 4

THE SOLUTION SECTOR

Charlton Park estate, Wiltshire, 10 October 1856. A night-time burglary of ten works of art, including *Virgin and Child with St Anne* (*c.*1503) by Leonardo da Vinci, leads to a desperate round of police interviews with locals who claim to have spotted a man 'at about six on the following morning, carrying two large parcels, loosely wrapped in brown paper, coming from the direction of Charlton Park'.[1]

Two years later and the estate puts forward a reward for the painting's recovery, or for any information leading to it. It works. After a London-based man comes forward to say that he had purchased the Leonardo da Vinci picture, an agreement is reached between him, a witness and the police, who subsequently arrange to meet and arrest the suspect.[2]

Fast forward to 1994 and the theft of two works by Turner, *Shade and Darkness: the Evening of the Deluge* and *Light and Colour (Goethe's Theory) – The Morning after the Deluge – Moses writing the Book of Genesis*, from an exhibition in the Schirn Kunsthalle, Frankfurt. The masterpieces were on loan from the UK's Tate Gallery and recovered in 2000 and 2002 respectively following a complex operation involving the police, the gallery's former Director of Programmes, Sandy Nairne, a hefty insurance payout of £24 million (Tate later bought back the insurer's title for £8 million prior to the works' recovery) and a fee for information reportedly totalling £3.2 million.[3]

Rewards, recoveries and intelligence: this amalgamation of intrigue continues to fascinate those interested in art crime. The examples above demonstrate that the fundamental process of recovering works has remained remarkably consistent throughout the centuries; that is, combined efforts made between the victim and law enforcement agencies, the use of rewards to draw out information, and the use of deception to catch out the criminals.

What has changed since early examples of art crime (not just art theft, but the breadth of offences discussed throughout this book) is the surrounding field of professionals now on hand to help prevent, detect and resolve issues. Rather than the neat partnership between the victim and police in our 19th-century art example above, today a sizeable commercial sector exists to investigate and advise in complex situations involving cultural property. This echoes a broader development of ancillary services around the trade in art, which has seen a proliferation of specialist advisers, insurers, handlers and lawyers specialising in cultural property, estimated to be worth €2.5 billion in 2006, in the European art market alone.[4]

Three key sections of these ancillary services will be discussed here in relation to art crime: private recovery options (including commercial databases for looted or stolen art, loss adjusters and private detectives); professionals concerned with justice or the resolution of cases (primarily art lawyers); and precautionary services (notably the broad range of advisory options on hand for buyers, to assist in reducing risk). Only a proportion of these professionals specialise in art crime alone, but all provide insight into how the issue is privately resolved in today's market.

If we are happy to view a growth in private art crime solutions partly as a reflection of broader developments in art world ancillary services, the increase can also be attributed to a lack of not-for-profit options (e.g. police stolen art databases rather than private alternatives) or, at least, the perception that these options are insufficient. The art market's increasingly close relationship with financial services and the use of art as an asset within a broader wealth portfolio have further accelerated demand for more systematic processes to assess risks linked to investments.

The sector's journey with private solutions to art crime has not always been smooth. Fundamentally, an additional layer of professionals or intermediaries disrupts direct relationships: between buyer and seller, between victim and criminal, between criminal and law enforcement agencies. This creates new opportunities for the ancillaries themselves to commit crimes, while also introducing ethical and legal boundaries for the professionals who are genuinely committed to stemming criminal activity.

There are no quantifiable means by which to accurately assess the positive impact that greater legal provision, advisory services and private companies specialising in art crime have had on reducing criminal activity in the sector. Nevertheless, the Art Loss Register has reported recoveries of more than 2000 cases in its first 25 years of existence;[5] and at least $700 million of Nazi-looted art is estimated to have been restituted between 2001 and 2006 alone,[6] primarily through private disputes led by lawyers; while the breadth and depth of services offered by art advisers to protect buyers' interests is expanding by the minute. It would seem that the art market has not yet outgrown the need for private remedies to its problems.

PRIVATE-SECTOR INVESTIGATION

If you crave an art crime experience crammed with covert meetings, dashes across Europe to verify intelligence and false identities, it would appear that the private sector is your best bet. As Charles Hill notes: 'For art crime investigation of the high-profile heist kind, apply imagination to your thinking and then direct it to direct action, without getting shot and killed along the way.'[7] While proactive and covert operations are carried out by police, the reality is that resources are often stretched or focused on other priorities (outside the investigation of crimes involving art).

The UK Council for the Prevention of Art Theft (CoPAT) was created in 1992, a charity that aimed to promote crime prevention throughout the art sector. The organisation continued the Internation Foundation for Art Research's practice of art crime bulletins, which dominated as the method of distributing information to the market about missing works prior to the advance of the Internet.

Independent agents poised to recover stolen art increased during the late 1990s, often with a background in the public sector. In the UK, former New Scotland Yard detective Charles Hill left the police to work with Nordstern Art Insurance in 1997,[8] later claiming that 'there is an increasing demand for private investigations of art crime because the police have largely withdrawn from this kind of work'.[9] Another former

UK police detective, Richard ('Dick') Ellis co-founded Art Management Group in 2005.[10] In the US, Robert Wittman, former senior investigator and founder of the FBI's art crime team, now practises as an art security consultant and has published on the subject, as has another former police officer from the FBI's unit, Thomas McShane.[11]

The majority of 'art detectives' openly discussing art crime with the world's media are private detectives, consultants or loss adjusters specialising in art. Both Ellis and Hill have since expressed frustration with the police's methods. In a 2013 interview with the *Financial Times*, Ellis described how 'He laments the short-termist, "parochial" attitudes to criminal investigations by police needing to meet government targets that means detectives no longer foster the kind of relationships that are built up over years.'[12] Hill has similarly described a 'parochial' attitude, in which:

> The Metropolitan Police, for example, have responsibility for crime investigation in London, a major city in the international art market. However, because of their parochial remits, major aspects of their law enforcement officers' work recovering stolen art need serious reconsideration.[13]

A passion for the chase, and the invaluable intelligence that private recovery professionals gather and often provide to police forces, makes them a crucial cog in the current mechanisms for recovering stolen art. Insurance companies, while wary of rewards, equally play a key role in recoveries – typically in considering the evidence and risk, but also providing funding for recovery efforts.

Private investigations, however, function within a legally complex field, one that has faced increasing scrutiny in recent years. One of the most controversial practices in the private recovery of art is the offer of rewards for information leading to the retrieval of a stolen item, a practice which is obviously not limited to the art world but has a long history within it: for example, the payment of a '300 marks' reward for the recovery of a Jan van Eyck work, stolen from a Berlin museum in 1877, which was delayed 'until [the authorities] have been enabled to test the truth of the finder's story'.[14]

The author and Emeritus Professor of Law John Smith has traced the UK's system for rewards back to the 17th century, where 'Statutes made provision for "parliamentary rewards" which could be claimed as a matter of right by any person who succeeded in bringing a criminal who was guilty of one of the specified offences to justice'.[15] Later, the Larceny Act 1916 tightened the rules by clarifying that payments should not be made to any individual linked to the original crime. Today, the law governing rewards in the UK is contained in the Theft Act 1968. In the US, there are limitations, and conditions to reward payments are governed on a state-by-state basis but generally require approval and contact with law enforcement agencies.

A distinction here should be noted between the terms 'reward' and 'buy-back'. An arrangement involving a 'buy-back' suggests that no prosecutions or further investigations will be pursued. Alternatively, the payment of a reward will not prevent further action or enquiries from the authorities.

Unfortunately, the provisions in place to ensure that rewards are not funding further crime do not provide a simple solution to complex situations. Determining whether an individual claiming the reward has a link to anyone involved in the original crime is rarely clear-cut, and while the majority of insurance companies, recovery agents and, indeed, the police have clear overarching policies on recovery procedures, situations are necessarily dealt with on a case-by-case basis.

If there is concern that while an individual did not directly commit the crime, he or she may be linked to the network of criminal activity, it remains challenging to prove that he or she knew or believed the items to be stolen goods and was 'dishonestly undertak[ing] or assist[ing] in their retention, removal, disposal or realisation by or for the benefit of another person, or . . . arrange[d] to do so', as specified in the 1968 Theft Act's definition of the crime of 'handling stolen goods'.[16] In other words, when it becomes apparent that an individual is attempting to sell items which they know are stolen, rather than merely providing information which could lead to stolen property's recovery, there is a risk of prosecution.

There have been cases where criminal intent has been identified during the process of returning a stolen work of art. In 2010, a solicitor and four other men were accused of extortion, following the recovery of a Leonardo da Vinci painting stolen from Drumlanrig Castle in Scotland in 2003. The prosecution ultimately failed to prove that the suspects had not alerted police with details of who had the painting and had attempted to make ransom demands.[17]

A year earlier, a retired UK solicitor, Anthony Blok, had been imprisoned for attempting to sell a painting worth £500,000 for a client, despite being aware that the work was stolen. The prosecution concluded that Blok had abused his professional position by hiding 'his client's identity and his involvement in this theft from the authorities', and he was charged with money laundering, perjury and perverting the course of justice.[18]

Determining whether an individual is linked to criminality naturally requires communication with law enforcement agencies, and efforts should also seek to confirm that the activities would not interrupt any ongoing police investigations. Nicholas Brett, previously Underwriting Director and now CEO of AXA Art Insurance, is clear on this:

> Loss adjusters employed by us do not go off on their own and start handing out rewards, meeting criminals, with packages of cash. The police could be looking at a much bigger picture than the specific bit of a gang's crime [than the insurance company] is interested in. You absolutely have to respect that. Sometimes you can be told to leave [the situation] alone.[19]

Checking that a potential recovery would not threaten pre-existing police operations is more of a challenge when working in cases abroad.

Not only are different jurisdictions involved, but police contact could be needed both in the country where the theft occurred and where the item is now believed to be.

The scale of the reward being offered can also cause debate. The aforementioned 2000 and 2002 recovery of two Turner paintings attracted criticism for the £3.5 million spent on recovery efforts (including a reward for information), which was questioned as being excessively high.[20] As Martin Bailey described the debate surrounding the payment, in the *Art Newspaper*: 'The most difficult ethical question is whether the £3.2 million payment for the recovery of the two Turners was right from the Tate's perspective – but damaging for the wider museum world.'[21] The current US$5 million reward up for grabs for information leading to the recovery of the paintings stolen from Boston's Isabella Stewart Gardner Museum in 1990 (see Introduction) has, however, received less criticism.

Criticism of financial rewards being set too high (or at all) is based on concern that they will indirectly encourage further crimes as criminals recognise the venture to be a profitable one. On the periphery of these ethical and legal debates around the use of rewards is the question as to whether cultural property should be an exception to general rules. That is, should conventional recovery rules and regulations be stretched if the objects at risk are considered 'unique' and 'irreplaceable'?

Criminals are known to have destroyed stolen or looted cultural artefacts when they have found themselves under pressure or at risk of being caught. For example, seven paintings (including works by Pablo Picasso and Claude Monet) stolen from the Kunsthal gallery in Rotterdam in 2012 were reported to have been burnt by the criminal's mother in Romania.[22] Other stolen paintings are dumped or abandoned shortly after the offence or, presumably, at the moment it dawns on the criminal just how famous the works are and how tricky they could prove to sell on. Two paintings, by Van Gogh and Monet, were reported to have been found in a car in Zurich, after being stolen from the city's Emil Georg Bührle Collection the week before.[23]

Julian Radcliffe of the Art Loss Register estimates that the proportion of stolen high-value paintings that will never be recovered could be as high as 15 per cent, because they have been hidden, damaged, lost or are 'too hot to hold'.[24] It is an argument also put forward by those collecting antiquities as a means to 'save' them from conflict – an argument which Professor Colin Renfrew argued against:

> Individual cases may be almost as painful as kidnapping: there is the temptation to 'save' the piece through purchase, just as to ransom a specific individual who has been kidnapped. But ultimately to reward the kidnapper or hostage taker is to fund the kidnapping process. To purchase the rare bird's egg of an endangered species is, directly or indirectly, to reward the exterminator.
>
> The single exception, and it is a difficult one, is that of the regional or national museum in the region or country of origin of the artefact (or, more accurately, of the region or country in which it was unearthed: archaeological context, and thus place of discovery, is the criterion).[25]

Regardless of whether you conceptualise the art market as two distinct parts (the legal versus the illegal, with a few fences in between) or as one – rather murky – whole, private agents recovering art works are in an ethically and legally fraught position. CEO of Art Recovery Chris Marinello, describes how, in this sector, 'it's important to get a reputation for doing things right – both ethically and legally. It may not always produce the fastest results but, long term, it encourages better relationships with the authorities and trust from clients and law enforcement.'[26]

THE JUSTICE SEEKERS

Cleaning up the aftermath of an art crime can be as costly and lengthy as solving it. Even in cases where the investigation and recovery of an art work runs smoothly, the trail of legal challenges, ethical debates and tangled interests can still prove a puzzle to unravel. Fortunately for many, there is an increasingly broad set of professionals on hand to help decipher situations.

The main companies recovering art (namely, the Art Loss Register and Art Recovery International) also offer services to support the recovery process once a work has been located. These services are focused on negotiation and discreet resolution, rather than simply a hunt for property. For example, Art Recovery describes on its website how 'The uncertain outcome, cost and publicity of litigation have left many looking for alternative means of dispute resolution. We have extensive experience negotiating high value settlements on behalf of claimants and good faith purchasers and have mediated multi-party disputes involving both single objects and large collections worldwide.'[27] Dedicated, often not-for-profit, organisations such as the Commission for Looted Art in Europe (set up in 2001), equally play an active role in representing victims at all stages of the recovery process: from the identification of looted works, to the negotiation of policies and procedures, to eventual recoveries.[28]

There is a body of lawyers specialising in cultural property disputes who play an instrumental role in reaching resolutions. Rather than a distinct body of law, lawyers dealing with art will deal with a broad spectrum of legal issues, including (but not comprehensively) criminal, tax, commercial, trust and intellectual property law.

Legal expert Stephen E. Weil traces the emergence of lawyers' interest in art to the late 1950s in the US, but says that it was 'not until 1971 that the American activity in this field began in earnest'.[29] He goes on to note that a graduate-level course dealing with art-related legal and ethical questions, offered in 1971 and run by Professors John Merryman and Albert Elsen of Stanford University, proved a watershed moment of the subject's later popularity, which was followed by a proliferation of research into the subject throughout the 1970s.

Research Lecturer Christa Roodt, of the University of Glasgow, describes how this interest developed: 'Since the 1990s commentators have argued in support of recognising cultural heritage law as a new or separate category of law,'[30] and there has been a proliferation of conferences concerned with art crime, including those organised by London's Institute of Art and Law and the annual Art Crime Conference run by the Association for Research into Crimes against Art (ARCA).[31] The Lawyers' Committee for Cultural Heritage Preservation, a not-for-profit organisation, has attracted 950 members since it was set up in 2007. Art lawyer Karen Sanig, of London-based Mischon de Reya, suggests caution in outlining an unprecedented boom, however: 'Art law has been around for ages – yes, it is receiving far greater media coverage but this attention is due to the huge leap in prices at the top end of the market, rather than a leap in the number of specialists.'[32]

As ever, litigation comes at a high price, a price that has invoked criticism against some working in the field of restitution. Lawyer Nathan Murphy describes how:

> Frequently, Holocaust survivors and their heirs are forced to turn around and auction away the very property they just recovered to pay those fees, and when representation is on a contingent fee basis and the recovered artwork is valued in the tens of millions or hundreds of millions of dollars, fees can be astronomical.[33]

An example in 2008 saw Marei von Saher sell *The Sacrifice of Iphigenia* (1671), by the 17th-century artist Jan Steen, reportedly to help pay back the 'millions in legal fees and expenses' accumulated during a nine-year restitution effort to recover the 200 Old Master paintings returned from her father-in-law, the art dealer Jacques Goudstikker.[34]

Given the option, the art market would prefer the resolution of its problems to be as secretive as its creation of them. The thought of a police unit breaking down doors of an auction saleroom is far less appealing to the trade than the presence of a lawyer with the right negotiation skills to make a problem go away. It is not a cheap solution, but it remains the more popular one.

THE PRECAUTIONARY TEAM

It is clearly preferable for an art crime never to have occurred than for it to be slickly resolved when it does. There is currently a growing sector of professionals within the art market offering to assess and reduce the risks incurred in entering a transaction involving cultural property.

Lawyers, art advisers, wealth management companies, stolen art databases, private art authentication services and insurance packages – these are just some of the options available to the buyers, sellers and collectors of cultural property to safeguard their objects, reputations and investments. Journalist Georgina Adam traces advice on offer for those purchasing art as far back as the 17th century, but recognises the 'extraordinary' power of top advisers today and the reality that collectors are 'so busy making money that they do not have time to run around a globalized art world'.[35]

The concept of presale due diligence is also expanding in both breadth and depth. No longer is a quick search online, or even search on a stolen art database, considered enough research to protect a buyer of art from future legal problems if an issue around its ownership, authenticity or condition later arises. Today, due diligence packages often include outlines of the methodology adopted within the research, as well as recommendations for further research.

This is partly a reflection of the growing number of buyers in the market looking at the investment potential of purchases and subsequently wanting to be sure of associated risks. It is also the result of legal cases where a lack of presale research has left buyers with little support from courts: for example, in a 2015 civil lawsuit brought by New York-based ACA Galleries against Joseph Kinney,[36] the latter was accused of having sold a fake painting, purporting to have been by the American artist Milton Avery, to the gallery. The judge's ruling against the buyer emphasised that there was a need to fully investigate a work's background and authenticity before money changes hands.

Lawyers (already discussed above, in relation to the resolution of disputes) play a crucial role in conducting due diligence services and giving advice on contracts prior to a client entering a transaction. This is part of a broader professionalisation of the art market, where records and contracts are increasingly used, often more due to the need to comply with tax obligations and improve business efficiency than from a desire to stem wrongdoing.

Art advisers and wealth-management experts also promise to reduce risks for their clients. The role and experience of these professionals is broad and they offer to cater for all steps of the transaction process: from selecting works, establishing the networks required to purchase them, and drawing up contracts, to moving and storing works, and the sale of any pieces. Subsequently, the 'risks' they work to reduce are often more commercially minded – that is, to do with the investment potential of a work, the use of art within loans and trusts and tax advice – than for the sake of avoiding becoming the victim of crime per se.

The outsourcing of advice, research or the brokering of transactions can lead to examples of misplaced trust and criminal opportunities. In 2015, the German art adviser Helge Achenbach was found guilty of 18 counts of fraud, through undisclosed 'mark-ups' between sellers and buyers.[37] Trusting another entity to purchase art and pool the investments on your behalf can be equally risky. In 2013 former US National Football League player Russell Allen Erxleben was arrested, accused of running a Ponzi scheme offering a non-existent opportunity to invest in a work by Paul Gauguin.[38]

Art historians, appraisers, authentication services and auction houses also play a role within the determination of facts prior to entering a transaction. This role aids the prevention of crime (e.g. by spotting any concerns with the provenance) but can lead to commercial disputes. In an uncomfortable case for Sotheby's London auction house in 2012, the owner of a painting sold through the auction house for under £50,000 subsequently discovered that the new owner had gone on to sell it as a work by Caravaggio with a somewhat more substantial £10 million price tag. Lancelot Thwaytes, the original owner, claimed that the auction house had been negligent in its formation of an opinion on the work's authenticity. The judge disagreed.[39]

Auction houses are not alone in facing lawsuits over decisions made on a work's authenticity. Chapter 2 has already mentioned the risks faced by art experts proffering opinions on the history or authenticity of a work of art. This is not a new problem: the art dealer Joseph Duveen was famously sued for slander in 1920 for questioning the authenticity of a work by Leonardo da Vinci.[40] More recently, in 1991, the art dealers Sean and Janet McNally initiated a civil lawsuit against the Metropolitan Museum of Art and the art historian James Yarnall, alleging that Yarnall made defamatory statements about them by challenging the authenticity of works said to have been created by the American artist.[41]

Authentication panels connected to artists' trusts or estates have been bombarded with civil lawsuits in recent years. The (now-closed) Andy Warhol Foundation was sued by Joe Simon-Whelan for conspiring to 'restrain and monopolise' the trade in the American artist's work. The case was eventually settled but caused substantial financial pressure for the Foundation, which announced in 2011 that it would be closing its authentication services early the following year, with the message that the move reflected 'the Foundation's intent to maximize its grant-making and other charitable activities in support of the visual arts'.[42] The Pollock-Krasner Foundation, which ran an authentication board for works by the American artist Jackson Pollock between 1990 and 1996, similarly faced lawsuits by individuals incensed that their works had not been authenticated.[43] The Keith Haring authentication committee (part of the Foundation), which oversaw work by the American artist, faced a lawsuit in 2014 from 20 owners of works rejected by the board;[44] by that time it had already disbanded its authentication services, in 2012, explaining in a press release that it felt 'the public and Foundation's charitable mission would be better served if the resources presently required for the operation of the authentication committee were redirected to purposes more directly related to the charitable goals'.[45] While legal action taken against authentication boards are again not criminal matters, the closure of, or limitations upon, risks services reduces one method by which the market can safeguard against and have an extra pair of eyes out for thefts and forgeries.

Insurance companies naturally have an interest in reducing the risk of loss, damage or fraud for their clients. For example, AXA Art Insurance runs a programme in 'risk prevention and research', entitled 'ARTPROTECT', which ranges from guidance on how to handle art work through to 'GRASP', a risk-assessment system to evaluate museum security systems.[46]

The security teams, equipment and consultants advising on the protection of cultural property within both private and not-for-profit collections and museums clearly have an impact on crime levels involving cultural property. Despite occasional spates of museum thefts in the UK and US, targeting museums in these countries is now a less viable option than in previous years or in alternative regions. This can partly be attributed to technological advances and specialist training. Improved communication between museums through groups such as the UK's London Museum Security Group, the National Museum Security Group and the American Alliance of Museums has boosted intelligence flow between institutions and their contact with police.

While many of the precautionary options available to buyers and sellers in the art market are concerned with protecting commercial interests (rather than guarding against crime), the role they play in detecting or deterring crime is key. Nevertheless, the art market is a world of limited visibility, and you need to ensure that your appointed navigator has your best interests at heart.

PROBLEMS WITH PROBLEM-SOLVERS

Art crime is often conceived as a problem that results (directly or indirectly) from a fundamental lack of sufficient regulation in the art world. It is an unfortunate irony that the professions emerging to help tackle and guard against such risks are often discussed as needing regulation themselves, or adding further opacity to the market and, in turn, opening up additional opportunities for crime.

Specialists and private agents working in the field of recovering stolen art tend to face the most scrutiny from those within the art world and the general public. Regulations are in place however. Loss adjusters in the UK do not have to seek an official licence, but the Financial Conduct Authority regulates those providing advice to insured parties (policyholders). Private investigators are also monitored, in accordance with the UK's Private Security Industry Act 2001, which outlines when a licence is required; and it is looking increasingly likely that the Security Industry Authority will be monitoring this sector in the future.[47] The majority of states in the US also demand that private investigators hold a licence and follow regulations, although these vary from state to state.

The regulation of art insurance comes under the broader regulation of the sector. In the UK, this is led by a division of the Bank of England entitled the Prudential Regulation Authority (PRA) and the Financial Conduct Authority. In the US it is regulated by state law and the Securities and Exchange Commission, and a broader National Association of Insurance Commissioners, which aims to standardise regulations by bringing together regulators from across the country. Likewise, art lawyers are heavily regulated by provisions in place for the profession in general. In the UK, this is managed by the Legal Services Board, an 'independent body responsible for the regulation of lawyers in England and Wales',[48] whereas the US has a more complex system due to the responsibility to regulate being placed within the government of each state.

Art advisers are monitored less. There have been attempts to tackle the additional risks that advisory services can bring to the field. By the 1980s the US had already seen the establishment of the Association of Professional Art Advisors (APAA) as, according to its executive Kimberly Maier:

> It was felt there needed to be standards and best practices established for the art advisory field. As collecting became more popular in the 1960s and 1970s, and the number of art advisers grew, there was need for an independent entity that promoted professional ethics and connoisseurship. The concerns had nothing to do with what [advisers] were charging. It was about transparency, and client representation, so that everyone in the chain knew what was happening.[49]

While trade bodies and codes of ethics exist for art advisers and consultants (see Chapter 6), there is not an independent governing body, equivalent to those monitoring advice provided on financial products. The quality of advice being offered to buyers and sellers within the art world can also be widely diverse. As noted by London-based adviser Emily Tsingou, in the *Art Newspaper*: 'A lot of young girls with gmail accounts can give art advisers a bad name.'[50] While education in this field has improved, with major auction houses Christie's and Sotheby's leading courses in art business, there is no effective or widespread method by which clients can determine the level of expertise being offered.

The inability to confirm a certain standard of expertise amongst art professionals is concerning for many, particularly new buyers with less experience upon which to make their own judgements about an investment or work of art. The inability to validate an individual's level of expertise is also a concern for those seeking opinion on a work's authenticity. The challenges faced by authentication panels have already been noted, while art experts and museum employees are increasingly aware of the need to set legal parameters prior to offering an opinion. There have been moves in New York to provide greater protection for both sides of an authentication. A piece of legislation proposed by the Art Law Committee of the New York City Bar Association looks to heighten the burden of evidence required in claims against art authenticators, which it defines as those 'recognised as having expertise regarding the artist for whom an opinion is sought, or having expertise in uncovering facts that serve as a direct basis for opinion as to authenticity'.[51]

The range of expertise and services being provided in the art market would make such a standardised assessment of professional standards ambitious to say the least. However, this reality means that sourcing the reliable advice, resources and professionals becomes yet another challenge for the buyer, collector or investor before being able to participate in an abstruse market, risk-free.

CONCLUSION

Investigating, solving and preventing art crime is not a domain for the public sector and law enforcement agencies alone. Due to the latter's insufficiencies or because the private sector is simply better equipped to deal with the peculiarities of the art sector, professionals are increasingly latching on to the business opportunities that art crime can provide. Of course, the private solution sector for art crime is not distinct from public efforts; indeed, the pair necessarily work closely together. Nevertheless, in an art market where a common language and knowing the 'right' people is still significant, art crime solutions embedded within broader ancillary services on offer are likely to be embraced more widely and prove more effective.

There are, however, risks to the solution to any area of criminality being dealt with through private means, in addition to fierce legal and ethical debate. Opportunities for further criminal activity can also be opened up by the fact that this solution sector creates an additional set of players within an already-tangled web of relationships set in an opaque environment.

Chapter 5

THE LEGAL LANDSCAPE

One of the first paintings I witnessed being recovered while I was at New Scotland Yard was René Magritte's *Les Reflets du Temps* (1927).[1] Having posed for a smug photo, the police officer and I walked over to load it into the Art & Antique Unit's vehicle – a small car, with back seats loaded with paperwork and not particularly accommodating for any painting, let alone a recovered treasure.

Ten minutes later (and following a debate over the standard of transport required to move art works), it likely dawned on the officer that it had been a mistake to bring someone with an art history background onto the team. It dawned on me just how large the gulf between the art world and law enforcement could sometimes seem.

Wariness between the art world and enforcement is, in part, a natural distance between two different sectors with little common language and few shared priorities. Part of the tension stems from a more fundamental gap, that between art and law in general. Those working in the art sector can be suspicious of a legal system which can feel as if it is unable to cope or fails to recognise the value (both financial and social) and lacks the understanding (conceptual, material or historical) of cultural property. This lack of understanding and appreciation of cultural property is often deemed to be the reason for the perceived paucity of official attention and resources dedicated to art crime.

If law enforcement agencies can, at times, be fairly accused of dismissing the art world as a lesser priority, the art world can be equally dismissive of attempts from law enforcement to intervene. Indeed, where law is applied, it is often accused of being too rigorous. Note the tone of a 2009 editorial headline in the *Art Newspaper* claiming that 'The Police Came Tromping into Tate Modern as Nosy Parkers', which reported the police's removal of Richard Prince's work *Spiritual America* (1983), depicting a naked ten-year-old Brooke Shields, from display in Tate Modern. Suggesting that the officers 'incorrectly' advised that the work was 'indecent', the article continued to mock the fact that they had been alerted by an exhibition advert: 'Who knew they were that culturally aware?'[2]

The balance, of course, would be an art world considered by all to be a legally compliant, well-regulated part of society, but one that is simultaneously able to support creativity and an adjoining economy. One of the challenges that legal systems seemingly have with the art market is that it is a world of flux. Not only is the cultural product itself constantly changing, both in terms of content and material, so too are the infrastructures and value systems linked to them.

The legal system's fondness for categorisations can fundamentally struggle with the slippery nature of the conceptualisation of art (i.e. what art is and is not) but also with the complex value systems which surround it. Law professor Lorenzo Casini cites Italian legal scholarship as pursuing an early legislative attempt to determine common elements within cultural property,[3] at the start of the 20th century, namely 'immateriality' and 'publicness'[4] (in terms of there being a public interest in culture's preservation and protection, rather than ownership). Early attempts to define these abstract qualities have not however stopped ongoing attempts to define cultural property, with pages of legislation crammed with lists of items covered and new determinations of the attributes which define cultural heritage. While the term 'cultural property' is still widely used, the term 'cultural heritage' is increasingly adopted in discussions, with UNESCO noting that property 'has a legal background (linked to "ownership"), while "heritage" stresses conservation and transfer from generation to generation'.[5]

Where a law does not detail art specifically, it is often left to be decided on a case-by-case basis, in court. Professor at Sotheby's Institute of Art Judith B. Prowda has explored the development of this trajectory and places emphasis on the words of Justice Oliver Wendell Holmes Jr in a 1903 ruling concerned with copyright in advertisements in the US, who advised that 'It would be a dangerous undertaking for persons trained only to the law to constitute themselves final judges of the worth of pictorial illustrations, outside of the narrowest and most obvious limits.'[6]

Due to the complexity and multitude of legislation that is relevant to an art world with an increasingly international remit, there can often be concern within the trade that an individual may 'accidentally' break the law. This fear typically emerges with the introduction of a new piece of law. When, for example, the UK's Draft Cultural Property (Armed Conflict) Bill 2008 was drawn up in a bid to ratify the 1954 Hague Convention, there was concern that there was only the need for prosecution to demonstrate a '"reason to suspect", rather than outright dishonesty'.[7]

For a sector to not possess a deep knowledge of all the laws that govern it is not unique to the art world. The question to consider throughout this chapter is whether the art market is creating too friendly an environment for criminal activity, and whether the professionals working within it have less knowledge than other sectors of how it should be behaving legally.

To answer such questions, it is worth considering whether the art market's typical behaviour or 'norms' comply with the legal frameworks relevant to it. The law and its application within courtrooms does, to some extent, consider market 'norms' or typical standards of behaviour within a sector, as a means to judge an individual or party's actions. A 2010 civil action against Simon C. Dickinson Ltd revealed that the London art dealer had entered into an agreement with another dealer, Luxembourg Art Ltd, to find a buyer for a Leonardo da Vinci drawing. The latter dealer had made an initial agreement to sell the work for the painting's owner. When the owner later discovered that the piece had sold for $1 million more than believed, and that this profit had been paid to Simon C. Dickinson Ltd (who the seller believed had instead been paid a portion of Luxembourg's fees), the party was keen to recover this additional profit.

The court did consider whether such an agreement was reasonable by considering the activity within the broader context of the art trade's practices: 'The person relying on it had to show that it was universally accepted by the particular trade or at the particular place, certain and not inconsistent with the express terms of the contract of agency.'[8] However the judge in fact rejected the suggestion that the practice was common and ruled that in any event it would not be acceptable without the seller's consent.

Courts have made it clear in their emphasis on the importance of behaviours such as due diligence that claiming a practice is widespread (e.g. that of selling paintings without a provenance) is not an excuse for wrongdoing.

There are limitations as to how far any legal system can involve itself in a market. In a 2008 US case, Joel Thome took civil action against the Calder Foundation, the private foundation responsible for overseeing the protection and interpretation of the work of American artist Alexander Calder (including the running of a catalogue raisonné to document all the artist's known works). Thome argued that he had been in direct contact with the artist about two theatrical stage sets and was frustrated at the foundation's decision not to authenticate or include them within the catalogue of Calder's approved works. He sought a court judgment to compel the foundation to authenticate the pieces. In a later appeal, the court maintained the earlier decision, finding 'no support for the proposition that our courts may by mandatory injunction affirmatively compel a private entity such as the Calder Foundation to include a particular work in its catalogue raisonné based solely on the court's independent finding that the work is authentic'.[9] It went on to point out that, regardless of the court's view on the work's authenticity, it would be unlikely to persuade the art market anyhow.

Getting to grips with the key pieces of law regularly used in and around the art market provides a foundation for further analysis of whether the art market lacks regulation. It also provides an insight into the sheer complexities that the often-clumsy relationship between art and law can bestow on art crime cases.

AN INTERNATIONAL HISTORY

Before considering the domestic legislation most frequently used to tackle art crime in the UK and US, it is worth looking at the broader platform of international law. Often referred to as 'soft law' or 'quasi-legal', international law is not always automatically legally binding. It is established or consolidated via conventions, treaties or agreed principles, in a bid to collate international principles which states agree to sustain (whether through the creation of specific domestic legislation, or the enforcement of existing laws).

The history of conflict in shaping international responses to cultural-property crime has been considered in Chapter 1, including the 1954 Hague Convention, which brought a commitment to protect cultural property in times of conflict and a second protocol (in 1999) to boost its clout by requiring member states to take steps to prosecute for 'serious violations'.[10] The US did not ratify this until 2009, while the UK has announced its intention to do so, but has not yet followed it through, stating in 2015 that it had 'run out of parliamentary time'.[11]

Continuing debate over how effective the 1954 Hague Convention is has not lessened the instrument's key role in signalling to the world that an international regime for cultural-property protection was on the agenda. That agenda has continued, notably with the 1970 UNESCO Convention on the Means of Prohibiting and Preventing the Illicit Import, Export and Transfer of Ownership of Cultural Property. This seminal agreement was adopted in Paris and promised a far broader scope in its protection of cultural property than the Hague Convention. Concern for the protection of cultural property was considered to be of importance in times of peace as well as conflict, and moves were made to urge states to tackle the illicit trade in cultural property by whatever means they have available. The convention is not retroactive, thus not applicable to items sold or transferred before 1970, a date now heard regularly in the art trade when considering the provenance of a work.

The comparative strength of the UNESCO Convention has ultimately been its vagueness. Nations are able to interpret which 'steps' to take to prevent illicit trade. The US was among the first to sign up, in 1972, and subsequently enacted its Cultural Property Implementation Act 1983, which reserved the US's right to refrain from a sweeping acceptance of other countries' export laws and to set up individual agreements with countries instead. Conversely, the UK was more concerned with the seemingly open interpretation of what 'culture' would be included. Nevertheless, having announced that it would use the definition of cultural property employed by the European Community (that is, a 'national treasure possessing artistic, historic or archaeological value'[12]), it ratified the UNESCO Convention in 2002.

If the 1970 UNESCO Convention is primarily concerned with the behaviour and legislation of states, the key international moment for private individuals who get caught up in cultural property disputes came with the 1995 UNIDROIT Convention on Stolen or Illegally Exported Cultural Objects. This international private law treaty was presented in Rome and supported the right to recovery for private individuals by aiming to facilitate the return of cultural objects. The convention is not retroactive, and recommends some form of compensation for individuals who are required to return objects but are considered to have conducted sufficient due diligence.

To date, the convention has failed to tempt the key market countries (countries in which demand for cultural property is conceived as higher than its role in supplying items for that market) into signatories – including the UK and the US. Concerns raised by the UK's Ministerial Advisory Panel on Illicit Trade, which published a report in 2000 on its considerations on illicit trade and means of reducing it, focused on the convention's limitation periods. The treaty proposed that the period a victim has to claim rediscovered stolen property before title is passed to a good-faith purchaser should begin from the time the victim has knowledge of the item's new whereabouts[13] – rather than an explicit obligation to seek out the stolen property.

These three key conventions are accompanied by numerous international and European agreements, which are either directly charged to protect culture and prevent crime against it, or which cover wider issues (e.g. money laundering) but have an impact on the art market. The Convention Concerning the Protection of World Cultural and Natural Heritage 1972, the EU Council Directive 93/7/EEC (now replaced by Directive 2014/60/EU) and a string of conventions devoted to restituting cultural property in the wake of Nazi atrocities (see the later section of this chapter on civil options) are some of the noteworthy agreements with culture at the heart of discussion. Meanwhile, agreements demonstrating the growing international consensus on the need to tackle organised crime have had a direct impact on the running of the art trade.

State decisions about which conventions or treaties to ratify can highlight the different priorities of market countries and source countries (where supply of cultural property is greater than domestic demand). While major market countries have demonstrated a tendency to support measures which will ensure trade in cultural property remains healthy, source countries have been quick to support measures with the greatest potential to prevent losses. The renowned academic Professor John Henry Merryman identified a polarisation of attitudes: the interest in 'nationalism' interest in cultural items (i.e. that cultural property should belong in its place of origin) and in 'internationalism' (i.e. items need protection for the benefit of the whole of 'humankind').[14]

It is important not to draw too absolute a line between these motivations. A desire to protect the trade in cultural property does not equate to a desire to protect illicit activity, just as a source country's desire to stop illicit trade does not equate to a desire to stop all trade in cultural property. Sweeping statements dividing those who wish to protect cultural property and crime around it from those who do not are increasingly difficult to make. Globalisation, and increased intergovernmental efforts to tackle crime and devastating learning curves around the role that attacks on culture can have on a society's identity, have all contributed to a more holistic and complex understanding of cultural property and obligations to protect it. Academics Francesco Francioni and James Gordley describe a situation in international law today, in which:

> Cultural property today can be seen as the object of individual rights, property rights, but also as 'communal property' or public patrimony, which is essential to the sentiment of belonging to a collective social body and to the transmission of this sentiment to future generations. In this sense, cultural heritage becomes an important dimension of human rights, in as much as it reflects the spiritual, religious, and cultural specificity of minorities and groups.[15]

CRIMINAL LAW

Art crime investigations do not arrive on the desks of authorities with a neat label announcing which law the offenders are breaking. Often a criminal case will have multiple layers of illegal activity that need unravelling, and it can prove as much a challenge to determine which jurisdiction the case falls under as it is to collate the evidence.

Solid understanding of the evidential requirements needed to prosecute for an art crime is often out of sync with popular understanding as to what constitutes an 'art crime'. Take, for example, a victim who has stumbled across a painting for sale which was stolen from them 30 years prior. The natural reaction for many would be to call the police. They, after all, may have records of the original crime, and perhaps seem best placed to seize the work from its current owners. Unfortunately, statutes of limitation periods and the absence of evidence, which is often the case after such a prolonged period (alongside the inability to track the original victims, in cases where another party has identified the property) mean that in many such scenarios the only action police are able to take is to provide advice on alternative options (e.g. civil proceedings). Similarly, some of the most influential art experts can still appear surprised to discover that their professional opinion on a work's authenticity is not necessarily sufficient evidence alone to prosecute.

Where a criminal-law route is available, the benefits for the market can be profound. In the UK, theft is covered by the Theft Act 1968; in the US, there are numerous federal laws dealing with theft and fraud, including the National Stolen Property Act. Prosecutors need to prove intent, or knowledge of wrongdoing, as well as evidence that the item was removed with the intention to 'permanently deprive' (i.e. not return at a later date). There are also offences of handling stolen goods, which is understood as attempts to gain monetary value from stolen property, disposing of it, or arranging to do so. To be convicted for handling or fencing, one must not be the original offender, i.e. the thief. The burden of proof is on the prosecution and is higher than in civil cases, moving from a 'balance of probabilities' to 'beyond a reasonable doubt'. The challenges of bringing together all of this evidence will be discussed in the later section of this chapter, on enforcement .

Establishing intent is equally key to the prosecution of fraud offences. Some individuals are confused when told that their proof that an art work is incorrect from an art-historical or material perspective is not necessarily sufficient. However, there is no criminal offence in possessing or creating a copy of an original art work, even if it possesses a signature that is not genuine. The criminal act is in the deception, perhaps at the moment a false signature is added with the intent to deceive a buyer, or the creation of a false story about a painting being discovered in your grandmother's attic, to mislead another.

The subtleties involved in establishing this intent to deceive were played out in a 1994 UK court ruling, in which Madame de Balkany sued Christie's auction house, after discovering a work purportedly by the Austrian artist Egon Schiele could be a forgery. While a civil case (rather than criminal), the case explored the point at which a painting could be considered a forgery: here, hinging on whether the heavy overpainting to the work had been done with the intention to deceive.

Although general restoration and changed character to the work could be deemed to be innocent, the court ruled that the extent of overpainting and the addition of a signature meant that the work had become a forgery. Christie's was asked to return the amount paid for the painting.[16]

Where the fraud has not been fully carried out or remains in the planning stages, it is still also possible to convict for 'conspiracy to defraud'. A number of high-profile criminal investigations have prosecuted for conspiracy charges, including the conviction of the UK art forger Shaun Greenhalgh for 17 years' worth of fake items – including the Amarna Princess, a forged statue purporting to have been made in ancient Egypt, which was bought by Bolton Council (for display at Bolton Museum) in 2003 for a reported £440,000,[17] and a number of fake Assyrian reliefs, falsely claimed to have come from Nineveh in Northern Iraq.

The fraudulent or anti-commercial behaviour of business organisations or individuals is less often included in discussions of art crime than, say, art forgeries or theft, but has historically enacted a major impact on the art sector when prosecutions have been successful. In the UK, the Competition Act 1998 prohibits agreements between businesses aimed at 'preventing, restricting or distorting competition',[18] while the Enterprise Act 2002 prevents engagement in a cartel. In the US, this area of criminality is tackled with three key pieces of legislation: the Sherman Antitrust Act 1890, the Clayton Act 1914 and the Federal Trade Commission Act 1914. The price-fixing investigation into two of the world's largest auction houses, Sotheby's and Christie's, which resulted in a £13 million fine for the former and, in the US (where price-fixing is a criminal offence), a further £5.4 million ($7.5 million) fine and the imprisonment of Sotheby's former chairman Alfred Taubman, remains the landmark example.[19]

Criminal damage cases tend to require less excruciating unpicking of events. The intent is often obvious: for example, with the politically motivated attack in London's National Gallery in 1914 on Diego Velázquez's erotic *Rokeby Venus* by a suffragette;[20] or, more recently, the systematic destruction of cultural property by the Islamist terrorist organisation Daesh in the Middle East.

While theft, fraud and criminal damage have dominated discussion of art crime for the majority of the latter's history, a (relatively) new kid on the block has the potential to dominate the subject in years to come: that is, money laundering. A term used to describe attempts to conceal the origin of money gained through illicit activity, money laundering is now one of the regular items on the agendas of international meetings of governments, as part of a broader international move against serious organised crime. The 1989 establishment of the Financial Action Task Force, an intergovernmental agency tasked with developing measures to combat the problem, reinforced this global commitment. International conventions – notably the Vienna Convention 1988, the Palermo Convention on Transnational Organised Crime 2000 and European Convention No.41, of 1990, on laundering, search, seizure and confiscation of proceeds of crime[21] – set the international tone on how the issue would be tackled.

In the US, the commitment to detect and prevent money laundering was put into action by legislation including the Money Laundering Control Act 1986, which established money laundering as a federal crime; the Bank Secrecy Act 1970, which required the finance industry to play an active role in detecting money laundering offences; and the later Obstruct Terrorism (USA PATRIOT) Act 2001, which extended enforcement tools to tackle activities linked to terrorism. In the UK, money-laundering regulations were devised in 1993, with later revisions in the Proceeds of Crime Act 2002 and Money Laundering Regulations 2003 (with amendments in 2007), and additional provisions in the Terrorism Act 2000, Anti-Terrorism, Crime and Security Act 2001[22] and the Counter-Terrorism Act 2008 (Schedule 7).

The legal professor Janet Ulph has pulled together a range of practical scenarios and examples of how money laundering could occur within the art market. Primarily, it would include anyone attempting to buy art as a means to launder money and 'Moreover, where a cultural object is stolen and sold to a foreign buyer, both the object and its sale price can be described as the "proceeds of crime".'[23] The impact that anti-money-laundering legislation could have on the art market is significant. Firstly, in the UK, all those dealing in quantities of cash over €10,000 (or an equivalent currency – the amount being specified in the EU Anti-Money Laundering Directive) will need to make enquiries into the provenance of that money. Secondly, businesses in regulated sectors now have a duty to report 'suspicious activity'.[24] There is thus no need for authorities to prove dishonest intent in a money-laundering case. Prosecution can occur for something you fail to do (i.e. report suspicious activity), rather than for actions you have undertaken. There is also an offence for 'tipping off' or for letting a subject who is linked to activity being treated as suspicious know (either deliberately or carelessly) that the authorities are being alerted.

Notable international cases involving money laundering and the art trade to date include the 271 artefacts which were stolen from the Corinth Museum in 1990 and recovered in a warehouse in Miami,[25] and the conviction of the Brazilian banker Edemar Cid Ferreira (discussed in Chapter 1).

The violation of export laws, which can be dealt with through criminal prosecutions or civil recoveries, is increasingly instrumental in disputes derived from the international nature of art trade and the wider implementation of patrimony laws. The UK's export licensing system is aligned to EU regulations and is guided by a Reviewing Committee on the Export of Works of Art and Objects of Cultural Interest, who work with the Department for Culture, Media and Sport.[26]

Notable controls on the import of cultural property include the UK's Dealing in Cultural Objects (Offences) Act 2003, which made it an offence to import (or acquire, dispose of or export) into the UK illegally removed cultural property (that is, illicitly removed property was now treated as stolen). In the US, Memorandums of Understanding (MOUs) are set up with countries where cultural items are under particular threat.[27]

The inclusion of cultural property within a broader set of sanctions against a country can suddenly make trade in a particular type of cultural property a criminal matter. The UN sanctions (Security Council resolution 1483) against Iraq and the subsequent sanctions imposed by the UK in 2003 meant that not only was it instantly a criminal offence to deal in items removed from Iraq after 1990, but it was an offence to fail to hand such items to a police officer. The US soon followed with its own measures in 2004.[28] Sanctions have been made for Syria in the UK, with its Export Control (Syria Sanctions) (Amendment) Order 2014, while the US is still waiting for a proposed bill to be passed.

This chapter can only hope to outline the major areas of legislation that will prove most familiar to anyone following art crime investigations. There are clearly many more types of criminal offences which can involve art, such as tax evasion, and crimes which the art itself is supposed to have committed – for example, offences under the UK's Obscene Publications Act (1959 and 1964), via content in contemporary art.

CIVIL OPTIONS

Criminal law is not the only, or indeed easiest, way to deal with wrongdoing in the art world. Where there is not the evidence, resources or circumstances to pursue criminal proceedings, civil options are available.

Cases resolved outside of criminal investigations or courts are not necessarily beyond the remit of discussion of 'art crime'. Civil action can be taken for a broad range of subjects: ownership disputes, attributions, restitutions, breaches of contracts, fraud and export cases are some of the more common. A portion of these disputes will have stemmed from criminal activity: for example, following a criminal trial, victims may seek damages; or else proceedings may help to resolve a situation deriving from a crime which occurred so long ago that criminal prosecution is no longer feasible (e.g. if a painting was stolen 40 years ago and the work has passed through numerous innocent hands since).

Civil lawsuits are also helpful in getting to grips with art market behaviour and better understanding ways in which criminal activity could work within it. For example, the opacity and types of business deals which lead to, and are uncovered within, a particular commercial dispute, can prove insightful of the environment in which trade is working. In turn, this can help understanding as to how crime could also function within the sector (e.g. by intentionally manipulating that opacity).

For victims of crimes involving cultural property, civil action can often be the preferred route even if criminal options are still available or ongoing. The fact that the action is being brought about by the victim (or the claimant), rather than a prosecution body, means that focus is on reaching a resolution through the allocation of damages or the return of an item. In addition to the lesser burden of proof required for civil cases, the resolutions are also typically reached faster.

One area of dispute in the art market which can often end up in a civil lawsuit is that of ownership. Both the US and UK common law legal systems follow the principle '*nemo dat quod non habet*' (a legal principle, translated as 'nobody gives what he doesn't have'), essentially bestowing the strongest ownership rights to the original owner of a stolen item. This differs to the civil-law system used in much of Europe, which provides greater rights to subsequent good-faith purchasers of a stolen item. Good-faith purchasers in both systems will typically be required to demonstrate this 'faith'. For example, in a 1997 lawsuit between Nicole de Préval and the antiques dealer Adrian Alan Ltd, the former was considered by a court to have conducted insufficient research or 'due diligence' prior to purchasing two 19th-century candelabra – which, it later turned out, had been stolen in the 1980s.[29]

There are exceptions to the owner's presumed right, the primary one being the 'doctrine of laches', or the consideration of any delay between the time a victim rediscovered an item stolen from them and a claim being made for it. In the US, there are variations around when this 'reasonable' time period should start. California, for example, starts the time from when the victim 'discovers' a work's location or the new owner, while in New York, the time runs from when the first 'demand' is made for a return of the item.

In the UK, there is a six-year statute of limitations period: that is, a claim must be made by the original owner within six years of its loss (unless the art work is still in the criminal's possession). The fact that these limitation periods differ across the globe can be exploited by criminals and can be a challenge for lawsuits, despite attempts such as the EU Council Directive 93/7/EEC of 15 March 1993[30] on the return of cultural objects (since replaced by Directive 2014/60/EU), which aimed to smooth the disparities between the jurisdictions of European Union Member States and aid the civil return of stolen cultural objects. The aforementioned UNIDROIT Convention of 1995 further aimed to smooth the process for private, civil recoveries.

Governments also use civil proceedings to resolve disputes over the recovery of items, or rather, a combination of criminal and civil proceedings. The US's Cultural Property Implementation Act 1983, which enables the government to return stolen items or works imported without the appropriate permission, is a civil forfeiture. The country's National Stolen Property Act is criminal but has the option for civil recoveries. Law professor Patty Gerstenblith has argued that the US government is increasingly moving towards a situation in which 'Whatever the reason, it may be that civil forfeiture has become a "replacement" for criminal prosecution.'[31] Civil recoveries and actions can also be made by courts following a criminal prosecution, through legal tools such as the UK's Proceeds of Crime Act 2002 which allows for the recovery of assets originating from criminal activity.

Cases calling for the restitution of items looted during the Second World War have consistently driven lawsuits in the art market since the 1990s. Key international conferences and agreements, including the 1997 London Conference on Nazi Gold, the 1998 Washington Conference on Holocaust-Era Assets, the 2000 Stockholm Declaration and the 2009 Terezin Declaration, have all called for swifter and fairer resolutions for those claiming an item's return. High profile cases included the 1997 success of the Rothschild heirs' claim to around US$40 million[32] worth of art and antiques from Austria, and Maria Altmann's long-fought battle – which she won in 2007 – to demonstrate her ownership of a painting by Gustav Klimt which was hung and celebrated in the nation's Belvedere gallery.

There was close international attention on the handling of these cases, and it was increasingly considered unacceptable to throw every conceivable legislative or bureaucratic hurdle in claims' way. The acknowledgement in a 2008 US-based case between Robert and Michael Vineberg (trustees of the estate of German Jewish art dealer Max Stern) and Maria-Louise Bissonnette (who had inherited a painting once owned by Stern) that 'forced sales', or sales which would not have been entered into voluntarily in other circumstances, should also be viewed as stolen, further paved the way for those seeking restitution.[33]

Civil-law cases also often derive from agency, or transactions in which there is an intermediary or fiduciary relationship, rather than a direct relationship between a buyer and seller. These relationships can further be complicated by the art market's fundamental and ongoing discomfort with putting contracts down in writing. In a 2010 lawsuit brought by the art collector Craig Robins against the David Zwirner (and David Zwirner Gallery), Robins alleged that the dealer 'reneged on a promise to sell certain paintings'[34] by South African artist Marlene Dumas. He claimed that the gallery had agreed to provide him with 'first choice' of Dumas's works (after museums, who seemingly had first selection) and to be removed from the artist's 'blacklist' of collectors. The attempt to get an injunction preventing the defendants from selling the works failed, and the plaintiff received a reminder from the judge to get a contract for the sale of goods.

Lawsuits claiming an abuse of a fiduciary responsibility also occur. A lengthy dispute in the 1970s, between those executing Rothko's will and his two children, saw the latter claim that the former had sold works at 'less than market value to favored clients while it collected inflated commissions'.[35] The executors were eventually fined and stopped from handling the estate further, but not until after a lengthy legal battle.

Civil disputes concerned with authenticity deal with express guarantees given at the time of the sale and the fine line between representation and misrepresentation (the term '*caveat emptor*' or 'let the buyer aware' still resonates loudly in the sector). To some extent, one has to be familiar with the art market to understand its terminology: someone entering the market for the first time could easily be confused by the phrase 'attributed to', which typically means that there are still questions around who created the work, or by the phrase 'in the style of', which again does not automatically equate to 'by the artist'. There is also an expectation for buyers to take the necessary steps to reassure themselves of the work's attribution before entering a transaction. For example, when William Foxley brought a claim for fraud (amongst other claims) against the auction house Sotheby's, alleging a work he had bought from them in the belief that it was by the American artist Mary Cassatt had turned out to be fake, a US court in 1995 placed the onus back on the plaintiff, partly for failing to have sought out the correct paperwork.[36]

The openness of lawsuits does remain a key dissuasion for many contemplating taking action. A lawsuit against the mega-gallerist Larry Gagosian (alongside Gagosian Gallery and Thompson Dean), filed by a collector Jan Cowles in 2012, claimed the dealer had sold her Roy Lichtenstein painting without prior consent.[37] Details from the case (which was later settled) were soon splashed across international media, including the *New York Times*, which considered how it was 'pulling back the curtain, if ever so slightly, on the way high-end deals are sometimes made in the contemporary art world'.[38]

SPECIALIST LEGISLATION

The legislation discussed to this point and used to prosecute the majority of major art crimes is not specifically designed to deal with art or cultural property. While on the one hand there may be reservations that creating specific laws to cater for this area in some way allows the sector to sit outside the rules imposed on general society, on the other hard such laws do tackle concerns that general law struggles to deal with the peculiarities of cultural property (e.g. its uniqueness, changing nature and complex value systems).

Legislation specifically designed to tackle issues surrounding cultural property tends to emerge in situations of crisis or where pre-existing laws appear insufficient for a particular situation. Often this can stem from obligations derived from international conventions which, themselves, can be specific in their scope (e.g. UNESCO's Convention for the Protection of the Underwater Cultural Heritage 2001, Convention on the Safeguarding of Intangible Cultural Heritage 2003 and Declaration concerning the Intentional Destruction of Cultural Heritage 2003).

The UK's Dealing in Cultural Objects (Offences) Act 2003 was created following the country's signing to UNESCO, in order to address a perceived gap in current legislation, whereby an item known to have been illicitly removed from another jurisdiction could have been openly sold on the UK market. The law closed this gap and created a new criminal offence applied to anyone who 'dishonestly deals in a cultural object that is tainted, knowing or believing that the object is tainted'.[39] 'Tainted' is understood as an item excavated or removed from a monument or other building or structure of historical, architectural, or archaeological interest, and such excavation or removal took place in the UK or elsewhere.

Similarly, the UK's Draft Heritage Bill 2008 was drawn up with the goal of filling a perceived gap, namely to better support the country's plans to ratify the Hague Convention (although this was not a requirement of its ratifying). The bill aimed to 'unify and simplify' the heritage protection system, but concerns were immediately raised over its ability to convict without any dishonesty needing to be evidenced, and it has progressed little from the initial draft.

Legislation focused on cultural property can also derive from external pressure from a particular group of society, rather than being prompted by a government's commitment to an international convention. There are a range of broad heritage and archaeological acts which have been supported by the archaeological community, for example the US's Archaeological Resources Protection Act 1979 and the UK's Ancient Monuments and Archaeological Areas Act of the same year. Others are even more specific: the US's Native American Graves Protection and Repatriation Act 1990 and the UK's Protection of Wrecks Act 1973. The UK's Treasure Act 1996 was a result of concern that potentially significant finds, and information about the context in which they had been uncovered, were being lost before being recorded.

The benefits of laws specifically designed to deal with cultural property are seemingly their ability to designate exactly what property the law is designed for, although each such law still faces the laborious task of outlining exactly what it considers to be 'cultural property'. The UK lawyer Pierre Valentin suggests: 'Specific legislation [for cultural property], if properly thought through is typically more tailored and its application to the art market more certain – therefore it makes it easier to manage the legal risks. General legislation can be difficult to apply to art, therefore the outcome of litigation can be more uncertain and legal risks are more difficult (and expensive) to manage.'[40]

Legislation tailored to cultural items does, however, arrive with its own problems and limitations. First, they can be harder to enforce – ironically due to the specificity. The very same specificity which aids investigations in some cases can prove to be the hurdle in other cases (e.g. if an act applies to an antiquity illicitly removed from a specific region, within a specific time frame, even archaeologists can struggle to prove this beyond doubt). A UK Select Committee reported in 2000 that:

> Since coming into effect the [EC Directive on the return of cultural objects] does not appear to have had the beneficial effects anticipated by Lord Renfrew or the adverse effects feared within the art market. The United Kingdom has not made or received requests for return of cultural objects under the Directive, nor

> is it aware of any other Member States receiving such a request, although the Government knew of one instance where return took place without recourse to the Directive's provisions. Some attributed the failure to use the Directive to the complexity of its provisions. Mr Richard Ellis, Managing Director of TRACE and a former head of the Metropolitan Police Art and Antiques Squad, attributed the Directive's non-use to the fact that it was cheaper and quicker to pursue a claim through the criminal code.[41]

Unsurprisingly, sector-specific legislation also has the effect of making a sector feel under attack. Simon Mackenzie's consideration of the impact of market behaviour following the implementation of the Dealing in Cultural Objects (Offences) Act 2003, which included a 'survey and a number of in-depth interviews with respondents in and around the London antiquities market' in 2007, found that 'there was a general feeling that the antiquities market was "under fire" from regulators, journalists and public opinion'.[42]

Sometimes this specificity is geographic, such as the UK's Kent County Council Bill 2001, which aimed to regulate the second-hand trade. Those supporting the Bill argued that as a national law was not going to be brought in any time soon, a regional solution could work.[43] The advice from the Ministerial Advisory Panel on Illicit Trade in 2000 was clear that while national law could be considered, a regional solution could prove more confusing than constructive:

> While we support the aim of these Bills, we are concerned about the piecemeal implementation of such private legislation, because this is likely to result in variations in regulatory régimes among different local authority areas. We believe that this could be extremely confusing and agree with the Parliamentary Committee's conclusion that 'the Government should reconsider

> the case for public legislation to regulate the market in second-hand goods' and that 'such legislation should be introduced at an early stage'.[44]

Where legislation is too specific – in terms of scope, time frame, geography or the categorisation of property – it can become more of a public awareness campaign or deterrent, than a means by which to increase the number of prosecutions. The importance of their success in raising awareness should not, however, be undervalued.

ENFORCEMENT AND EFFECTS

A larger number of laws dealing with cultural property will be of little effect if they are not enforced. The limitations of resources allocated to law enforcement agencies (see Chapter 4) is clearly one reason why there may not be a high level of convictions under a particular law. The way that the law is written will equally affect how 'enforceable' it is: that is, the evidential requirements required to prosecute under it and how applicable this is to cultural property and crime in the art market.

One of the most frequent evidential challenges ahead of any attempt to convict for a crime involving cultural property is proving exactly what the item of cultural property is. From looted antiquities, where even the most specialist archaeologist may be unable to determine definitively the exact origin, to the struggles in proving authenticity, 'black-and-white' answers are hard to come by in the art market.

Proving criminal intent can also be difficult in a sector where there are no strict 'tick-boxes' or universal processes – even determining whether an individual has knowingly bought a stolen item could require an assessment of numerous factors, including their knowledge of the property involved, the buyer's experience of the market and whether any suspicious factors (such as an abnormally low price) were displayed by the seller. Sometimes, of course, proving dishonesty proves an easier task: presumably the officers who uncovered the British art dealer Jonathan Tokeley-Parry's method of disguising Egyptian antiquities as gaudy tourist [fakes][45] had little trouble proving that this was an attempt to hide the object's true nature.

The transnational nature of the art market also brings challenges to enforcement. Determining which jurisdiction applies in disputes (with suspects and victims often in different countries) is time-consuming and causes tensions due to variances in nations' stances on statute of limitations, tax infrastructures, categorisations or financial thresholds of cultural property protected and import/export provisions. A famous case in the 1980s, brought by William Winkworth, who had a collection of Japanese netsuke stolen from him, against the individual who had later bought the items not knowing they were stolen and the auction house Christie's, where they were subsequently consigned for sale, explored the principle of *lex situs* – that is, the jurisdiction of the country in which the object is currently located will be prioritised. The judge ruled that regardless of where the items had been stolen (England) and were now being sold, Italian law should nevertheless be applied as that was where they were sold to a good-faith purchaser (who had obtained good title).[46]

While intergovernmental agencies, primarily INTERPOL and Europol, aid the process of enquiries and communication channels, there is no international court for art related disputes to rule on differing opinions and the tensions which can emerge from differing jurisdictions.

The increasing relevance of foreign laws in domestic courts has heightened the need for trade to be more aware of the international context. This is particularly important in the US, where a series of cases have enforced foreign patrimony laws (that is, using a foreign country's definition of what is stolen property, rather than a domestic definition). In *United States v. McClain* (1977 and 1979), several dealers were convicted for conspiring to bring in antiquities from Mexico, considered 'stolen' under Mexico's patrimony laws.[47] A later case, beginning in 2002, concerned the US antiquities dealer Frederick Schultz, who was later imprisoned for conspiring to deal in antiquities deemed stolen under a foreign country's (Egypt's) patrimony laws.[48]

The opaque nature of the art market further complicates investigations. Professor [at Sotheby's Institute of Art] Judith B. Prowda summarises the 'typical art theft', featuring 'the classic Eternal Triangle of the Law: an honest man [A], a rascal [B], and another honest man [C]. Typically, the rascal imposes upon both of them . . . and leaves to the law the problem of deciding which of them shall bear the loss.'[49] Such a triangle becomes more complex in a trade where art typically passes through multiple hands before any concerns were raised.

When law enforcement has committed time and resources to investigating a crime, there is no guarantee that the prosecution services will consider the case to be in the public's interest to pursue. When an art crime does reach a trial, prosecution lawyers may not possess expertise in the subject matter and court decisions on cases involving art have been historically unpredictable in terms of outcome. For example, despite a body of examples in which courts have refrained from directly ruling on the authenticity of art work (see the discussion of the case involving the Calder Foundation, earlier in this chapter), in a 2012 civil lawsuit a UK court ruled that a painting purportedly by Russian artist Boris Kustodiev, and sold by Christie's auction house to Viktor Vekselberg, was a fake and that the auction house should return the cost of the work, in addition to the claimant's court fees.[50]

This inconsistency of outcomes can also be linked to the academic Alessandro Checi's point that 'cultural heritage law lacks specific and effective procedures for the resolution of disputes', a key reason why alternative dispute settlements (e.g. arbitration and mediation) are often preferred options. Subsequently, he argues that 'This ad hoc fashion of dealing with cultural heritage disputes entails that the final settlement mostly depends on the choice of the forum and of the applicable law (outcome-determinative nature of forum selection), which often depends on the arbitrary circumstance of where an object is discovered.'[51]

CONCLUSION

A key question to ask when considering the efficacy of a legal system to tackle criminality in the art market is what role we are expecting the system to play. Is the hope that law and its enforcement will successfully tackle all criminal activity in the sector, act as a deterrent, and transform the behaviour of professionals in the art world? Or is the goal simply to raise awareness of criminality in the art market?

The academic Derek Fincham reinforces the need to consider the limitations of law's influence: 'Many cultural heritage advocates argue for more laws, often overestimating the ability of law to eliminate looting and theft.'[52] As evidenced throughout this chapter, the ability to prosecute and deter criminal activity is dependent on a web of factors including law enforcement resources, evidential requirements and the harmonisation of distinct jurisdictions.

In reality, legislation specifically designed to protect cultural property and prevent its use in criminal activity is at its most useful as an awareness-raising exercise or as a deterrent. Conversely, it is the internationally prioritised, broader drives against pan-sector crime (for example, money laundering) which could have the most impact on the art market's behaviour, in terms of resources allocated to tackling the issue, intergovernmental working and prosecutions.

While there are particular challenges in law's interaction with cultural property, it is inaccurate to claim that those working with cultural property are free from legal boundaries. If the art sector is accused of being 'unregulated', the law, at least, is pulling its weight.

Chapter 6

THE NEXT STEP?

Hot on the heels of claims that art crime is an increasing problem are assertions that something needs to be done about it. Generally, that 'something' is focused on the art market, a sector which is widely perceived as fundamentally welcoming to wrongdoing. Is it time for the art market to change? If so, what would such change look like?

Demands for tighter scrutiny of the art market, as a means to tackle crime, have a history. Mounting pressure to stem demand for looted antiquities, primarily from the archaeological community, has been building since the late 1960s. By the 1990s, the criminologist John E. Conklin had made a direct link between art crime and the 'social organisation' of the industry in which: 'Like art itself and the value attached to that art, art crime is the product of collective action, an outcome of interactions and networks established in the art world for legitimate purposes.'[1]

Today, the majority of remedies put forward to tackle art crime maintain this emphasis on the need to change art market behaviour and are dominated by calls for 'transparency' and 'regulation'. This pair of somewhat sweeping terms will be considered in greater detail below, alongside a range of solutions currently being discussed to combat art crime.

Considering proposals for solutions to art crime will not explain why a solution is being sought nor whether now is the correct time for art crime to be tackled. The motivations of those seeking solutions can be understood as an amalgamation of ethical reasons, external pressure from the public and the financial benefits that a more efficient and transparent trade could offer. However, these motives for change are worth considering throughout. The solutions which satisfy the widest cross-sector of motives are likely to be the most promising.

GREATER REGULATION

The art market is frequently and increasingly described as 'unregulated'. There is less discussion about how such regulation could or should look.

The term 'regulation' can be used to refer to a multitude of measures applied to a sector. Discussion of regulation and the art market tends to focus on the industry's ability to regulate itself (e.g. via trade associations), the option of a licensing body (where registration is required to practise a profession and demonstrate a statutory level of capability to work in a particular role) or the establishment of an external body to apply additional rules and scrutiny (e.g. a governmental organisation).

Scrutiny from the government has occurred sporadically in the art market's history. Legislation against auction 'rings', where dealers agree to keep bids low and then agree a purchase between themselves, was introduced in the UK 1927,[2] and both the UK and the US have legislated against 'bid-rigging', where agreements around bidding are made before the sale.[3] A 1985 investigation by New York's Department of Consumer Affairs placed a greater spotlight onto auction house practices. Instigated with 'a view of finding whether there was rampant abuse',[4] the conclusion drawn by the report found that this was, in fact, not the case.

A further appraisal of the New York auction houses was sparked by revelations that Sotheby's 1987 sale of Van Gogh's *Irises* (1889), to entrepreneur Alan Bond, was made feasible by the auction house's loan of $27 million to assist the buyer in the purchase (total price $53.9 million).[5] By funding a large proportion of the sale, it was felt the auction house was unfair and misleading the market, and a subsequent public hearing questioned a broader set of art market practices, including secret reserves.

Isolated cases of government's brushes with the art market give a very limited view of how 'regulated' the sector is. The breadth of legislation discussed in the previous chapter may be more indicative of the frameworks in place; indeed, the UK law practice Constantine Cannon has estimated that 167 laws and regulations alone are currently monitoring the British art market.

The art market is, nevertheless, predominately self-regulated: that is, while there are rules and laws to obey, the sector is in charge of ensuring that they are obeyed. Voluntary trade associations and adjoining codes of practice have long played a central role in the US and UK sector. Dealers' associations include the British Antiques Dealers' Association (BADA, set up in 1918), the Society of London Art Dealers (in 1932), the Association of Art and Antiques Dealers (LAPADA, in 1974), the Art Dealers Association of America (in 1984), CINOA, an international art and antique dealers voluntary organisation (in 1987), the International Association of Dealers in Ancient Art (in 1993) and the British Art Market Federation (in 1996). The majority have since set up codes of practice to which they expect members to adhere.

Auctioneers and art advisers equally have members-only associations, namely: the Society of Fine Art Auctioneers and Valuers (SOFAA, founded in 1973); the National Association of Valuers and Auctioneers (NAVA, in 1988), which includes valuers and auctioneers from multiple sectors including plant and machinery, property and art and antiques; and the Association of Professional Art Advisors (APAA, in 1980). Further codes of conduct for the trade have been provided by UK's Code of Practice for the Control of International Trading in Works of Art (in 1985) and the Council for the Prevention of Art Theft (in 1999).

Museums, libraries and archives have gone to great pains to prepare their own guidance and codes of ethics, which outline principles on acquisition, borrowing and restitution of items, where appropriate. These include codes of practice from the International Community of Museums (code of ethics issued in 2004), the UK's Department for Culture, Media and Sport (due diligence guidelines, in 2003) and the Museums Association Code of Ethics (first introduced in 1977, and since updated).

These codes of conduct vary and are, of course, concerned with matters outside of crime alone. However, they generally emphasise the need to conduct due diligence on cultural property (in terms of authenticity and stolen goods), to not trade or accept stolen or illicitly removed items and to prevent conflicts of interest. The process of joining and staying within an association is equally seen as a means to ensure a certain standard and consistency of behaviour across the sector.

Art and antiques dealers at the upper end of the market typically undergo a form of peer review. This can take the form of vetting of their objects by museum professionals or other members of the trade at art or antiques fairs or as part of the assessment procedures required for membership of trade bodies. In the latter, fellow professionals or existing members of trade associations can be asked to comment on the knowledge and experience of applicants. While this may lack external objectivity, the Secretary General from the British Antique Dealers' Association, Mark Dodgson, comments: 'Dealers who comment on another's membership are independent of one another. In fact, strictly speaking they represent one another's competition, and they would not want to encourage membership of their trade body by a dealer with a bad reputation who does not have a track record of legitimate sales, since by associating with them it would damage their own reputation.'[6]

The effectiveness of associations on the regulation of behaviour of those involved in the art market is hard to judge. Seemingly, the suspension or removal of a member from art market trade associations is a rare occurrence. Rebecca Davies, Chief Executive of LAPADA (the Association of Art and Antiques Dealers), explains: 'We deal with a dozen a year, and 95% end amicably. The situation is normally a result of miscommunication or a missing piece of paperwork [rather than criminal activity].'[7] Similarly, the Secretary General of CINOA, Erika Bochereau, says she has 'worked at [the organisation] for 10 years and cannot remember a situation that hasn't been resolved or was escalated to our board'.[8] Whether this low level of indiscretions reflects a lack of widespread breaches of codes of practice, or rather a lack of indiscretions being effectively identified, remains debatable. It should, however, be noted that dealers' love of gossiping about one another and their tremendous memory of art works on the market tends to act as one of the most effective self-regulating systems in the art market.

The art market has driven the development of its self-regulation beyond trade associations. The creation of the Art Loss Register was supported by auction houses, among other investors, there is now greater inclusion of provenance details in auction catalogues, and professionals from the sector have played a crucial role in the development of legislation, including the Dealing in Cultural Objects (Offences) Act 2003. Christie's aforementioned decision to stop selling antiquities lacking a pre-2000 provenance (see Chapter 3) was also an example of key players in the sector taking a lead to stem the sale of illicitly removed items.

Unsurprisingly, self-regulation is more effective when there continues to be an element of external pressure or scrutiny. Erin Thompson, Assistant Professor of Art Crime at the City University of New York's John Jay College, has considered the self-regulatory structures devised by American museums, in relation to objects with a questionable provenance. The research found that the American Alliance of Museums (AAM) and the Association of Art Museum Directors (AAMD) were more effective in the self-regulatory regime surrounding Nazi-looted art, where public pressure and scrutiny was intense, compared to the less effective compliance in relation to looted antiquities.[9]

The next level of regulation up from self-regulation discussed in relation to the art market, i.e. the licensing of professionals or compulsory registering with a professional body, tends to focus on 'art advisers' in the art market (as noted in Chapter 4). Unlike advisers in other high-risk markets, notably those advising in the finance sector, there is no licensing required to be an art adviser, nor a standardisation of qualifications. Subsequently, while the upper end of the art market provides opportunities to invest comparable sizes of money to those investing in a purely financial product, the advice provided will not be regulated (as it would be with the latter). This is comparable to other sectors, including real estate. While one would expect a mortgage adviser to be regulated, this is because it is advice on the financial product involved in buying the house, not advice on which house to buy.

Financial products linked to art objects are not automatically regulated under broader codes imposed by the UK's Financial Conduct Authority (FCA) and the US's Securities and Exchange Commission (SEC). The regulation of investment schemes is dependent upon the structure of the fund, rather than the type of asset involved.[10] Typically the structures of art investment funds are not those that would require regulation, although the recently launched Cadell+Co in London promises to be 'the first independent specialist to provide FCA-regualted portfolio management expertise for art in trust'[11] – and others are following in its footsteps.

In the UK, art funds can also be subject to new regulations introduced to ensure that unregulated collective investment schemes (i.e. not directly registered or monitored by the FCA) were limited in promoting their products to sophisticated investors, 'described as having "extensive" investment experience, or high-net-worth individuals, defined as having an annual income of more than £100,000 or investable net assets of more than £250,000'.[12] France has also taken action to protect those contemplating potentially risky art investment. The country's financial market regulator, the Autorité des Marchés Financiers (AMF), issued a statement in 2011 warning the public of an art investment company, Marble Art Invest, which was proposing 'an investment in works of art, claiming guaranteed yields of 4% per quarter, or over 16% per annum . . . The AMF wishes to remind those investors who might be attracted by this offer that such a high rate of return, although guaranteed, is unrealistic in the light of current interest rate levels.'[13] Twenty individuals involved in selling the products were later fined a collective €3.8 million by the regulator.[14]

Auction houses and valuers also fall within broader laws and regulatory bodies. The Uniform Commercial Code, a US-wide 'code of commerce', guides many of the states' laws on auction houses, includes provisions of a warranty of title by sellers to buyers, in addition to the fact that more than 20 states in the country also require a licence for auctioneers, including New York. Publicly listed companies within the art market, notably Sotheby's, are required to publish financial information and adhere to regulations. The valuation of art for tax purposes is also monitored, in the US by its Internal Revenue Service, which may refer to its Art Advisory Panel for a review of values submitted and, in the UK, overseen by Her Majesty's Revenue & Customs (HMRC).

The art market could, of course, be more regulated. Many of the proposals for greater scrutiny are intertwined with calls for greater transparency (see the following section of this chapter) or with the creation of an independent body to aid the resolution of disputes – as with the property ombudsman, an alternative dispute mechanism, which offers advice on disputes between agents and clients.

Hesitation from the art market over the prospect of more regulation does not mean that the proliferation of criminal activity within the sector is preferred. Apprehension can equally derive from concern that regulation (or overregulation) could create burdensome bureaucracy, the displacement of trade to regulation-free zones and ultimately damage to an economy which plays a crucial role in many countries. There are examples that regulation can have a negative effect. The economist Clare McAndrew describes the prominence of New York and London as the key art centres in the 1950s and 1960s in part due to 'a new system of taxes on art sales and other regulatory deterrents that drove buyers and sellers away from France to more liberal trading regimes'.[15] Ongoing debate over the impact of the Artists' Resale Right Regulations that were introduced in 2006 on the UK's art market, while not concerned with art crime, demonstrates the concern felt by the trade over shifts in legislation. In a 2014 report, the British Art Market Federation considered the levy with an examination of the Contemporary and Modern sectors of the market, noting that UK trade fell by 22 per cent between 2008 and 2013, compared to the US's growth of 70 per cent in the same period.[16]

Regulation could however make the art market a more sound market, as well as one with a greater ethical and legal reputation. As the market becomes more international and closer in proximity to the finance sector (as art is increasingly appreciated as an investment within a mixed portfolio of assets and for its greater role within alternative financial services, such as leverage for a loan), regulation may organically become more appealing. Adriano Picinati di Torcello, Director of Art and Finance in the consultancy firm Deloitte Luxembourg, argues that 'Sectors with high levels of trust and security, attract high levels of investment. As the art market continues to attract new audiences and there is wider circulation of art works across the globe, it will make sense to search to mitigate the inherent risks of the art market by a push towards more self-regulation.'[17]

GREATER TRANSPARENCY

When do suspicions around a market emerge and calls for regulation increase? When it is 'murky' or, rather, when people do not know everything going on within it and have no easy means of finding out.

Transparency, or rather a lack of transparency in the art market, is a key focus for its critics. As with many of the sectors under attack in today's political scrutiny of widespread corruption and prioritisation of business ethics, there is suspicion that secrecy equates to wrongdoing. As Stephan Kuhn of EY Tax Insights has observed: 'Transparency may well be the watchword of our times. Leaders promise it; voters and shareholders demand it.'[18]

The art market can definitely lay claim to its own style of murkiness. From hidden prices and undisclosed identities of buyers and sellers, to vague histories and details of the objects being sold; secrecy is the cornerstone to much of the sector's practices. The levels to which art market players will go to retain this secrecy can be seen in the US art collector Marguerite Hoffman's lawsuit against a financier, David Martinez, and L&M Arts gallery for failing to keep her sale of a work by the American artist Mark Rothko a secret.[19] Legal disputes over the authenticity and ownership of works of art also continue to be resolved behind closed doors.

The price of items being sold was more challenging to uncover when dealers made up the majority of the market. With the rising prominence of the auction houses since the late 1980s, a larger proportion of art is sold in public salerooms, and auction data is now available online via services such as artnet (albeit typically for a small fee). The prices which are released by the auction house do not always give the full picture, however. Fees charged to the consigner and buyer, which can be as high as 25 per cent, are mostly but not always included. Equally discreet is the realm of secret reserves and guarantees (where a third party has a financial interest in the work) which lurk beneath the figures.

Secrecy around the identities of those involved in a transaction, combined with the highly subjective and dynamic value of cultural property, can lead to fears of market manipulation. In a world dominated by networks and the understanding that art is not sold to simply anyone and everyone, both buyers and sellers use intermediaries to source, buy and sell works of art. Secrecy on both sides (the buyer and seller) gives the intermediary a lot of power. An ongoing (at the time of writing) criminal investigation into the freeport billionaire Yves Bouvier, in 2015, for claims of fraud and money laundering saw the internationally known market figure accused of allegedly taking unauthorised mark-ups from sales of art to the Russian oligarch Dmitry Rybolovlev, while acting as an intermediary.[20]

In addition to concerns about price manipulations, there can be a lack of transparency around the role that professionals are assuming and potential conflicts of interest, which could result in commercial dispute, but also create opportunities for criminal activity. The art lawyer Pierre Valentin highlights the need for clarity: 'The point is that the professional seller may sell as principal or he may sell as agent for the owner. If he sells as principal, he sells as the owner and the money he makes is a profit. If he sells as an agent, he owes the owner fiduciary duties (e.g. to account for secret profits) and the money he makes on the sale is a commission. The problem comes if the professional seller does not clarify in which capacity he acts. This, in turn, can cause confusion in the mind of both sellers and buyers.'[21]

Opportunities for manipulation within an environment of blurred identity is likely to increase as ownership structures become more complex within the art world, due to the rise of art funds, pooled investment schemes, shell companies and the opportunity to keep art works in freeports (tax-friendly zones). Insider trading, where individuals gain access to information before the public and use this knowledge to their financial benefit, also thrives within opaque environments. The art market journalist and author Melanie Gerlis has noted this practice as an art market norm, describing how 'dealers regularly bid at auction on works by the artists they represent, adding a public value to their stock'.[22]

A ruling by the State Supreme Court in New York caused panic amongst the sector in 2012, when it threatened to shake up this system of hidden players. A dispute over an unpaid bid for a 19th-century Russian enamel box, valued at $460,000, at William J. Jenack auction house in New York, ended up in a court ruling that auction houses would be obliged to reveal consigner details to buyers. The judge noted that the 'buyer was not obliged to pay, since a legally binding contract must include the names of both the buyer and the seller'.[23] Despite a shudder of panic throughout the sector (although, in reality, the details would only be provided to the buyer and only then in the instance of a payment not being made) the ruling incurred little real change as it was later reversed.

Anti-money-laundering legislation has forced the sector to be more open. The need to report suspicious activity has nurtured a greater feeling of obligation to identify both the identity of the client but also, if large amounts of cash are used, the source of their funds. Most major auction houses now have anti-money-laundering departments.

The history of the art for sale in the market is as controversial as the players and finance surrounding it. Understanding [of] the importance of due diligence – that is, asking the right questions to check that the object is what it pertains to be and is legally acceptable to sell – is gaining ground. However, the lack of sufficient tools (namely a comprehensive stolen art database, as discussed in the following section of this chapter) means that the processes and level of due diligence undertaken are inconsistent and largely dependent on the monetary value of the item involved (i.e. less extensive checks will be undertaken for items of lesser value). Museums are feeling the pressure to open up their own data, and a series of online databases of public collections and their known provenance are increasingly becoming the norm. Auction houses are equally devoting greater resources to researching the history of lots.

The degree to which the art market relies on transparency to succeed is tricky to establish. Secrecy can be desired for reasons outside wrongdoing. The old saying that auctions were fuelled by the three 'D's' – debt, death and divorce – introduces a host of other sensitive situations where secrecy may be preferred. One person's transparency could be another person's invasion of privacy. Invading the privacy of a criminal, without disrupting this broader respect for the market, is perhaps the balance being sought.

THE DATABASE DREAM

If there remains disagreement as to the cause of the art world's problems with criminal activity, there is surprising consensus over one of the proposed solutions: an all-singing, all-dancing stolen art database. The dream consists of a service that not only collates international records of stolen art onto a publicly accessible, user-friendly platform, but in which known fakes are also recorded.

The dream is not a new one, and attempts have been made to turn it into reality. The history of police stolen art databases in the UK begins in 1974, when London's Metropolitan Police Service started its card index system which, by 2002, the Art & Antiques Unit had relaunched as a computerised system, known as the Stolen Art Database. In addition to the option to upload images of the property, core details of the victims, the place where the offence occurred and any known modus operandi (the method of a criminal operation, e.g. a night-time burglary) could also be included to enable the database to further serve as an investigative tool. Initially, this system was conceived as one that could be accessed by other police forces around the UK, but today it remains that forces report relevant crimes to the London squad, who then assess it prior to uploading details manually. In the US, the FBI's National Stolen Art File (NSAF) database was upgraded in 1998 to include additional investigative data.

The NSAF database has a price restriction on the items recorded, of at least $2,000 (or less if linked to a major crime), and requires that objects be 'uniquely identifiable and have historical or artistic significance';[24] the UK's Stolen Art Database, meanwhile, places emphasis purely on items being unique and identifiable. This focus on items being identifiable is not an attempt to determine whether an item is of particular value, but rather a practical acknowledgement that while, for example, a Meissen vase may be of high monetary value, there could be numerous examples of the same model. From an evidential perspective, this would become hugely problematic to prove, beyond all reasonable doubt, as being the victim's item.

Attempts to collate national databases into one publicly funded international resource have failed to reach aspirations. The database created by the international police organisation INTERPOL in 1995 aimed to establish an intergovernmental tool, but access to the resource is limited to those working in law enforcement and again relies on nations' law enforcement informing INTERPOL of losses, rather than automatically uploading from the national systems.

Pressure and attempts to update police databases have come from academics, government and the art market itself. The need for a database is a regular feature of international treaties and recommendations on stolen art. The UK's 2000 Advisory Panel on Illicit Trade proposed 'the institution of a specialist national database of unlawfully removed cultural objects',[25] which was followed up by the establishment of a Home Office working party to progress a national database, working with commercial operators. By June the following year, the group had been disbanded and described as 'ineffective' because 'participation of the commercial sector prevented the consideration of all options and compromised any resulting competitive tender'.[26] The Police Information Technology Organisation (PITO) was asked to review options, which have continued back and forth until today – where official attempts to design and fund the resource remain undecided.

Private-sector alternatives have moved to fill this lack of public solution (as discussed in Chapter 4), notably the Art Loss Register and Art Recovery International. Both work closely with the police and include items registered as stolen with police onto their databases, as well as other issues potential buyers may desire to discover during the due diligence phase – including issues over ownership or known damage. Subsectors within the market also run their own systems to monitor and alert professionals about stolen items. London's Assay Office, set up in 1939, maintains a record of items considered forged or stolen,[27] while UK stately homes run a 'hotline' and circulate known risks via email.[28] The databases are not solely used by the trade. In 2014, the rough breakdown of the Art Loss Register's 380,000 paid searches was as follows:

- 300,000 were for auction houses
- 45,000 were for 'individuals, museums, police, customs, etc.'
- 25,000 were for art fairs, i.e. dealers
- 10,000 were for dealers outside of art fairs [29]

There are currently a multitude of options available when attempting to conduct due diligence: private stolen art databases, looted art registers, authentication bodies, online research or just a decent set of questions for the seller. To some extent, this system allows the buyer flexibility in determining what level of research is justified for an item – based on its price, object type and the context in which it is being bought (e.g. is it in an auction house where diligence processes are underway, or are you buying it out of the back of someone's van?). On the other hand, such a range of research options has reduced the efficiency of any of them. Rather than a 'one-stop-shop' service which allows the individual conducting due diligence to be reasonably confident that if the item were stolen, it would be listed, individuals are having to consult multiple resources prior to entering a transaction.

A further problem of current database options is their accessibility, or rather the lack of accessibility. While it is argued that private databases' charges are minimal, or at least affordable, the existence of any cost is prohibitive. Requesting a search on the Art Loss Register can cost around £60. Immediately that rules out the likelihood of any item worth less (or much more) than this amount being checked against records.

A public-private option – that is, an amalgamation of police and private databases – may promise to balance the need for resources on the former's behalf, and the credibility and depth of data from the latter's. Such a partnership would introduce its own challenges, however, including the management of transferring victim data to a commercial entity.

Given that there is so much support for a comprehensive database, why do demands for a new database or for a revision of pre-existing services fail to progress? Fundamentally, a business model to suit all parties involved has not been found.

GREATER AWARENESS AND UNDERSTANDING

One of the more optimistic methods proposed to tackle criminal activity in the art market is the raising of awareness of the problem, its impact and the expected standards of behaviour in the sector. Essentially, this is an argument to improve the use of the current structure and systems, rather than a proposal to overhaul the entire market's infrastructure and behaviours. The strategy also includes a range of target audiences: the art market, enforcement agencies, the general public and criminals (these groupings, as ever, are not mutually exclusive).

One theory is that raising awareness of crime within the art market (among both buyers and sellers) would cause crime levels to slow down. This thought process derives from a belief that if more professionals understood the risks of crime (including risks to themselves if linked to criminal activity), fewer would get involved or ignore the problem. The academic Simon Mackenzie has considered a 'market reduction approach', in which buyers would be 'made to care about the origin of their purchases, and not only to reject looted antiquities, but also to report suspicions to the police when they have them'.[30] This is to be achieved through public education campaigns, with the hope that buyers may eventually turn to less 'problematic' luxury goods.

Educating buyers within the art market, particularly those with lesser knowledge of the sector and the art work itself, would certainly reduce the risk of purchasing fake, stolen or looted items. This need is more pronounced at the lower end of the market and with items bought online, where there is a greater proportion of buyers entering the market for the first time. In a world dominated by subtleties in language, knowing the difference between works 'attributed' to an artist and works 'by' an artist could prevent costly mistakes. The Object ID system, set up by the J. Paul Getty Trust in 1993, established a new standardised method of recording works of art, a crucial tool for those encouraging owners of art to create better inventories of their collections to increase chances of recovery if anything were stolen.

A greater awareness of victims' rights if something does go wrong is evidently needed. The UK's Illicit Trade Advisory Panel noted that greater awareness was needed of buyers' rights under the Sales of Goods Act 1979, and of their ability to challenge sellers if the latter refuse to guarantee title or quiet possession (that is, possession without another's claim of ownership of a piece), while also advocating that the government fund an education drive to raise awareness of illicit trade.[31]

The International Council of Museums (ICOM) has adopted an awareness-raising approach in its publication and circulation of 'red lists', a collection of information about cultural property considered under threat, with visuals to aid enforcement and dealers to identify illicitly removed items. Where new legislation has been introduced, trade associations have equally adopted an educative approach by publishing guidance for its members, for example the British Art Market Federation's 'Anti-Money Laundering' guidelines (2000).[32] International conventions have equally prioritised the need for broader education about the risks, including the UNESCO Convention of 1970 (article 5), which includes the requirement for states to implement 'educational programmes to develop respect for cultural heritage.'[33]

Recommendations for greater specialist understanding of art crime within law enforcement has long been dominated by a notion that police officers working in units solely devoted to art crime should possess a certain passion for art history. This romanticised version of an 'art detective' is misleading. It is far more useful to understand the application of law to the art market and comprehend the sector's practices, than it is to have the ability to talk convincingly, for example, of Pablo Picasso's Blue Period (although the latter may assist in building those crucial relationships with the sector). For enforcement officers not working in art alone, specialist training and raising awareness of stolen art databases available to them is useful. This strategy has been used with success in times of conflict: following the invasion of Iraq in 2003, customs officials received training in the types of antiquities to look out for, while military personnel in Iraq were provided with playing cards illustrated with cultural monuments in the region to boost their awareness and reduce accidental losses.

Educating criminals as to the impact of their offences and actions on the historical and social value of cultural property has been put forward as a method to dissuade future offences. The academic Dario Gamboni has argued that 'what is needed to curb art vandalism is more art education . . . so as to minimise the resentment that stems from their incomprehension of such symbolic representations'.[34] English Heritage (now Historic England) also placed education at the heart of its attempts to reduce reoffending rates against cultural heritage, advocating engagement with the perpetrator in a bid 'to ensure that they are aware of the consequences of their actions, have the opportunity to make reparation, and agree a plan for their restoration in the community'.[35]

There is a tension underlying some of these recommendations for greater awareness and education, at least among those pushing for greater awareness within the market. We would be underestimating those in the market by suggesting that they are unaware of how crime functions within the sector they work in. If anything, the trade itself holds the information to best determine the most effective solutions.

A CARROT AND STICK

If the art world is often considered as an unruly sector of today's society, proposals to bring it into line veer from greater punishment to the incentivising of better behaviour.

The perceived wisdom is that punishment acts as a deterrent to crime. Whether punishment arrives in the form of punitive criminal sentencing or the humiliation of a messy civil lawsuit, the high importance of reputation for those working within the art market suggests that this is an effective approach to stem crime. For those not working as professionals in the trade, for example art forgers selling art online, the threat of a sentence could be less effective.

The effect of the deterrent is likely based on how severe the punishment is and how likely a person is to get caught. In terms of the severity of punishment, we have already seen in Chapter 2 that despite harsher sentencing guidelines (namely the US Sentencing Commission's 2002 amendments), variations in different jurisdictions' approaches and the interpretation of law in courts has led to a pretty inconsistent message to criminals in terms of sentences. The strongest punishments tend to be given when cultural property is caught up within organised criminal activity. While UK theft, for example, carries a maximum sentence of seven years' imprisonment, anti-money-laundering legislation can result in up to 14 years' jail time (in the US, this can be as high as 20 years). The fact that governments are more committed to devoting enforcement resources to tackle organised crime and money laundering, than art crime per se, also makes the likelihood of conviction in these activities greater and thus the deterrent more effective.

Part of the punishment is the ongoing damage to an individual or business's reputation. The academic Derek Finch argues that this could have a stronger impact if actions were more broadly felt. Considering the widespread shift in museums' attitudes towards purchasing antiquities lacking a pre-1970 provenance, he concludes: 'The impetus for this collective shift has been a gradual shaming of many museums. Shame will affect behaviour when moral disapproval of the community at large impacts the collective actions of individuals.'[36] An apprehension of being caught out would certainly explain the recent wave of restitutions following the investigation into the US dealer Subhash Kapoor who, at the time of writing, remains charged in India with allegedly smuggling more than $100 million worth of antiquities and selling them to collectors and institutions. Internal museum investigations are underway, with items already being returned including an 11th-century bronze sculpture from the Asian Civilisations Museum in Singapore, seven objects from the Honolulu Museum of Art and two items from the Art Gallery of New South Wales.[37]

The repatriation of items on a voluntary basis (i.e. through a negotiation process rather than it being enforced) can result in compensation for the former owner. Michael Ward's return of the Aidonia Treasure, a collection of Mycenaean (late Bronze Age) jewellery, which his gallery had bought in 1993, to Greece resulted in a private settlement in which he reportedly received a 'substantial' tax deduction.[38] Having demonstrated his good faith, the negotiation was deemed a favourable solution to both parties, while others have argued that despite rewarding behaviour (i.e. returning items believed to have been looted), such a strategy does not deter similar future purchases being made.

Compensation is again a core component of the private returns of cultural property supported by the 1995 UNIDROIT Convention and the UK's Portable Antiquities Scheme, which essentially encourages people to come forward with found items by offering monetary compensation for property later established as treasure and thus owned by the state.

At present, there is very little real deterrent to committing crime in and around the art market. The challenges of prosecuting crimes involving cultural property (discussed in Chapter 5) make the chances of getting caught out relatively small. The rewards for good behaviour are also underdeveloped and more focused on incentivising good behaviour after a situation of wrongdoing has been identified (e.g. the repatriation of a looted item), rather than incentivising good behaviour in the first instance.

CONCLUSION

The majority of solutions proposed to tackle art crime presume that the art market is either directly, or indirectly, the root of the problem.

The fact that the art market itself has historically been the key driver for many of the changes to its practices and regulation is often overlooked. Key art market players and trade bodies have played an influential role in the progression of specialist legislation and advocating for greater law enforcement resources.

A presumption that the art market's current claim of self-regulation is merely lip-service may have an element of truth within it, but it is equally apparent that criminal activity is fundamentally against the interest of the art market (on an individual, business and sector-wide basis). The reason why the sector has not faced greater regulation the past is debatable: perhaps influential members of society are protective of its current ways of working, perhaps the research is just not sizeable enough to demand attention, perhaps the government is simply uninterested. Nevertheless, today's political climate for cracking down on organised crime and corruption in the higher echelons of society could mark a change in the sector's formerly peaceful life.

The sector's increasing proximity to that of the financial services could make regulation more tempting on a business level. Whether the art market needs to be exposed, watched more closely, better equipped to facilitate good behaviour (e.g. a database), encouraged or punished, it is unlikely to do so until this is clearly in its own interest. This publication argues that this day is ever approaching.

CONCLUSION

Anthony Browne, of the British Art Market Federation, once reflected: 'I have heard some say that just because someone is super rich, he must be up to something shady. It doesn't occur to them, apparently, that people can become rich through honest toil and that people who are not super rich have an equal capacity to behave dishonestly.'[1]

This book partly started out as an attempt to work out my own thoughts on the art market and behaviour within it. Was it as crooked as it could seem when working at New Scotland Yard, or as misunderstood as it could sometimes feel when working closely with art dealers as a journalist?

The problem with such a quest is that, with no quantifiable means by which to determine how many professionals are tempted into criminal activity and how this compares to other markets, any sweeping conclusion of art market behaviour only ever seems to be based on a foundation of snapshots, gut feeling and anecdotes. What has emerged as a more interesting question is whether the art market's fundamental infrastructures, business practices and attitudes are directly or indirectly permitting criminal activity. The watchwords for this question are 'transparency' and 'regulation', or rather the lack of both, which many perceive to be the root of problems for the sector.

The exploration of the opportunities, impacts and solutions for art crime in today's art market has consistently demanded recognition of the fact that it is a market much changed since consideration of 'art crime' as a topic began. Yes, there are still tight networks, secrets and probably more than its fair share of massive scandals, but it is increasingly apparent that it is simply not good business sense (on an individual, business or sector-wide basis) for the trade to act in a way which leaves it open for crime or adjoining allegations. This is partly because of the broadening awareness of art's potential as an investment and buyers beginning to demand greater understanding of risks, and partly a reflection of a broader social and political moment in society, in which governments worldwide are increasingly demanding greater scrutiny of business behaviours. The litigious routes market players are prepared to take to resolve situations are also acting as a deterrent.

Of course, criminal activity still occurs, often in a pretty large-scale and high-profile way. But, if we started out asking if the market is the root to its own evil? The answer can only really be that it is hard to definitively say. It is, however, clear that efforts to work with the art market on its own development are likely to be the most effective means by which to close down opportunities for criminal activity (whether by supporting its own efforts or through seeking its advice on external measures). In other words, the art market could well be the route to its own solutions.

NOTES

INTRODUCTION

1. Mackenzie and Green 2009, p.151. Almost 90 art dealers responded to the survey, which aimed to analyse the impact of the UK's Dealing in Cultural Objects (Offences) Act 2003 on the antiquities market. The question of 'bad apples' was not specifically included within the survey and thus the authors ventured that 'Given that this response was unprompted, we suggest that the "bad apples" opinion carries significant weight in a diagnosis of the trade's relationship with the looting problem.'
2. Gapper and Aspden 2015.
3. Noted and discussed in greater detail in Bazley 2010, p.125.
4. Adams 1974, p.9.
5. The FBI did not follow suit until 2004.
6. From over 12 countries, details available at: http://www.lootedartcommission.com/NFVHQY50452.
7. Bazley 2010, p.84.
8. Still cited on the FBI Art Theft Program page, although it is unclear to whom it attributes this figure. Available at: https://www.fbi.gov/news/videos/fbi-art-theft-program.
9. http://www.interpol.int/Crime-areas/Works-of-art/Frequently-asked-questions. This has been noted and considered in greater depth in Durney 2013.
10. Sandra Calvani, 'Frequency and figures of organized crime in art and antiquities', in Manacorda (ed.) 2009, p.30.
11. Conklin 1994, p.134.
12. Tijhuis 2006, p.1.
13. BBC News May 2008.
14. INTERPOL describes organised crime as: 'typically involved in many different types of criminal activity spanning several countries. These activities may include trafficking in humans, illicit goods, weapons and drugs, armed robbery,

counterfeiting and money laundering' (http://www.interpol.int/Crime-areas/Organized-crime/Organized-crime).

15 Discussed in greater detail in Simon Mackenzie, 'The market as criminal and criminals in the market: Reducing opportunities for organised crime in the international antiquities market', in Manacorda and Chappell (eds) 2011, p.72.

16 Alder 1999.

CHAPTER 1

1 Farouk Dougui, Jabey Bathurst and Simohamed Rahmoun were found guilty for conspiracy to defraud, following a trial at Isleworth Crown Court in 2013. Further details available in D'Arcy 2013.

2 Fakes and forgeries are also combined with genuine items within the movement of stolen and illicitly removed goods.

3 Telephone interview with the author, November 2014.

4 According to Janet Ulph, 'Introduction', in Ulph and Smith 2012, p.30.

5 Commission for Looted Art in Europe [undated].

6 UNESCO 2015.

7 As discussed by Ana Vrdoljak, 'Enforcement of restitution of cultural heritage through peace agreements', in Francioni and Gordley 2013, p.23. This is also considered in Van der Auwera 2013.

8 Reported by Shaheen 2015.

9 Mowat 1994, pp 1–2.

10 Riedlmayer 2007, p.108.

11 Email conversation with author, January 2015.

12 MutualArt staff 2011.

13 Jolly, David, 'Authenticity of Painting Questioned in Capture of Serbian', July 21 2011, New York Times, www.nytimes.com/2011/07/22/world/europe/22iht-serbia22.html?_r=0

14 Radosavljevic 2014. The conviction was subsequently quashed in 2015.

15 Baumel 1993.

16 Cases detailed on the United Nations International Criminal Tribunal for the former Yugoslavia. Available at: http://www.icty.org/action/cases/4

17 Petrovic 2013, p.52.

18 As noted by Frulli 2005.

19 Zimonjic 2001.

20 Email conversation with the author, February 2015.

21 Pryor January 2012.

22 Hill 2008.

23 [As reported in] Pryor January 2012.
24 Interview with the author, December 2011.
25 Doland 2013.
26 Lemerick 1928.
27 Conklin 1994, p66.
28 Rogoff 2015.
29 Parry 2012.
30 Further discussed in Campbell 2015.
31 McAndrew 2012.
32 McAndrew 2014.
33 Jones 2013.
34 US Attorney's Office 2009.
35 Guo undated, p2.
36 Wang Yunxia, 'Enforcing import restrictions on China's cultural objects: The Sino-US Memorandum of Understanding', in Francioni and Gordley (eds) 2013, p.241.
37 UNESCO 2011.
38 Noce 2015.
39 Tyler 2014.
40 Association of Chief Police Officers 2013, p.5.
41 Harrington 2000.
42 Beech 2003.
43 Dutra 2004, p.89.
44 Reuters 2014.
45 Keohane 2015.
46 Oster 2012. He was jailed and later released.
47 ATG Reporter 2012.
48 *Sevenoaks Chronicle and Kentish Advertiser* 1899.
49 Karczewski 2015.
50 Christie's 2012.
51 McAndrew 2015.
52 Hiscox 2014, Introduction.
53 Walton 2007.
54 Williams 2006, p.20.
55 Statement provided for article, Pryor January 2013.
56 Interview with the author, April 2015.

CHAPTER 2

1 'The Metropolitan Police Service's Investigation of Fakes and Forgeries', Victoria and Albert Museum, London, 23 January to 7 February 2010.
2 McAndrew 2015.
3 Martinez 2015.
4 Bazley 2010, p.27.
5 Historic England 2013, p.5. Heritage crime is understood as 'any offence which harms the value of England's heritage assets and their settings to this and future generations.'
6 Conversation with the author, November 2015.
7 Hirst 2010.
8 For example, Iain Robertson, head of Art Business Studies at Sotheby's Institute of Art, discusses art as a passion investment in an interview, available at: http://www.sothebys.com/en/news-video/blogs/all-blogs/degrees-of-distinction/2013/10/art-investment-sothebys-institute-iain-robertson.html
9 McAndrew 2011, Foreword, p.5.
10 Scheerhout 2009.
11 Parsons 2011.
12 Gordon 2010.
13 BBC News 26 July 2007.
14 Pryor September 2012.
15 [Quote provided to author for article] Pryor September 2012.
16 Valentin 2013.
17 For further information on the Lagrange lawsuit, see *Lagrange v. Knoedler Gallery*, no.11-cv-8757 (S.D.N.Y., filed 1 December 2011); settled in 2012.
18 For further information, see *United States v. Wiseman*, no.89-CR-00125 (D. Haw. 1989), aff'd, 991 F.2d 804 (9th Cir. 1993).
19 While author and art crime expert Noah Charney writes that the 'The largest victim of art crime is the art trade', he goes on to say that 'crimes of deceit and forgery affect the art market in a generally beneficial way. The members of the art trade, galleries, auction houses, dealers, middle men, and sellers all benefit, earning money even if the item they are handling is not what they claim it be. Only the buyers suffer, perhaps over-paying for a fake or misrepresented work of art.' In Charney 2009, pp 107 and 109.
20 Boroff and Freifeld 2010.
21 *Telegraph* 2011. Hobbs denied any wrongdoing.
22 *Gov't of Islamic Repub. of Iran v. The Barakat Galleries Ltd.*, [2007] EWHC 705 (Q.B.D. 2007), rev'd by [2007] EWCA Civ. 1374 (A.C. 2007).
23 McAndrew 2011, p.16.

24 Kessenides 2010.
25 Telephone conversation with the author, November 2014.
26 Vogel, Carol, 'Sotheby's Moves its Antiquities sales to New York', *The New York Times*, July 23 1997, www.nytimes.com/1997/07/23/arts/sotheby-s-moves-its-antiquities-sales-to-new-york.html
27 A spokesperson for the auction house notes that this figure includes results from one of its 'Exceptional sales' and so does not reflect the normal volume of Antiquities or totals handled annually.
28 *Republic of Croatia v. Trustee of the Marquess of Northampton 1987 Settlement*, (N.Y. Sup. Ct. 18 November 1993) (jury verdict dismissing all claims), aff'd, 203 A.D.2d 167 (N.Y. App. Div. 21 April 1994), aff'd, appeal denied, 84 N.Y.2d 805 (N.Y. Ct. App. 22 September 1994), damage award aff'd, 232 A.D.2d 216 (N.Y. App. Div. 1996).
29 Associated Press 2007.
30 From a 1940 *Newsweek* article, noted in Esterow 2005. There have been historical variations on the saying.
31 Coomber 2013, p.2.
32 *Art Newspaper* 1991.
33 Brodie, Doole and Watson 2000, p.11.
34 Others have argued that the study of forgeries can be an enlightening pursuit in itself, for example former Victoria and Albert Museum director Mark Jones considers justifications for studying fakes, both to help avoid future mistakes in authentication and as 'evidence of the changing value structures of those directly involved. It is evident that faking is itself an index of the value of the objects faked.' Jones (ed.) 1992, pp 8–9.
35 *Chicago Tribune* 2005.
36 British Art Market Federation/Arts Economics 2015, p.2.
37 McAndrew 2015.
38 Interview with the author, June 2012.
39 Charney 2009.
40 Figures from, Brodie, Doole and Watson 2000, p.13.
41 United States Sentencing Commission 2002.
42 Pears 2011.
43 Pryor, February 2013.
44 Salisbury and Sujo 2010, p.239.

CHAPTER 3

1 Sale, '20th-Century British Art', Sotheby's, London, 25 May 2011.

2 According to an Art Loss Register spokesperson, the painting was identified by the Government Art Collection, and the Art Loss Register handled its subsequent recovery, which was completed in September 2013. See also Pryor 2011. There was no suggestion of theft, simply that the painting was missing.

3 'Illicit Trade in Antiquities', House of Commons Debate,26 May 2004, vol 421 cc458-82WH. Available at: http://hansard.millbanksystems.com/westminster_hall/2004/may/26/illicit-trade-in-antiquities#S6CV0421P1_20040526_WH_50

4 Norman 1996.

5 Interview with the author, April 2014.

6 Adams 1974, p.11. The formation of the Unit was also in response to a series of thefts targeting stamp dealers: see Chappell and Hufnagel (eds) 2014, p.195.

7 From the FBI's website. Available at: https://www.fbi.gov/about-us/investigate/vc_majorthefts/arttheft

8 House of Lords, 20 February 2007. Available at: http://www.publications.parliament.uk/pa/ld200607/ldhansrd/text/70220-0001.htm

9 Association of Chief Police Officers 2013.

10 Though its official remit is London, the Metropolitan Police Service's Art & Antiques Unit deals with national and international crimes, because London is the key portal for criminal activity involving art, the works involved often emerging or being sold there.

11 The US had a dedicated Customs Art Fraud Investigation Center between 2000 and 2004. The team was disbanded following the attacks on the World Trade Center. As reported in 'US Customs redeploys its art investigators', *Art Newspaper*, no.143, January 2004. Since 2007, the Cultural Property, Art and Antiquities Investigations (CPAA) team was established within the customs department.

12 Evans 2014.

13 Lewis 2015.

14 Every UK police force which the author felt would feasibly hold relevant data was sent a Freedom of Information Request, requesting data of crimes involving 'art' or 'antiques', between March 2014 and 2015.

15 Telephone conversation with the author, November 2015.

16 Conklin 1994, p.279.

17 Vitelli 2000.

18 For example, the work of Clemency Coggins on illicit trade in Pre-Columbian antiquities, in 1969.

19 Efrat 2009, p.5.

20 As referenced at: http://www.sccjr.ac.uk/projects/the-international-market-in-illicit-antiquities/
21 Davis 2011.
22 Pryor and Gerlis 2011.
23 Office for National Statistics 2015.
24 *Liverpool Mercury* 1895.
25 As noted in Efrat 2009.
26 Shabi 2015.
27 Gill and Hull 2007.
28 *Spiegel* online 2012.
29 Pogrebin and Flynn 2013.
30 Interview with the author, March 2015.
31 Authentication processes are, of course, not solely focused on catching crimes: misattributions, workshop productions and over-restoration are also considerations.
32 Telephone interview with the author, November 2014.
33 Noah Charney, 'Art crime in North America', in Chappell and Hufnagel (eds) 2014, p.211.
34 Committee for Cultural Policy 2014.
35 Numerous media reports, including Binnie 2015.
36 At the time of publication this case was still ongoing. As reported in Milliard 2014. Wildenstein denies the charges.

CHAPTER 4

1 *Morpeth Herald* 1858.
2 Ibid. For further details around the reward, see *Devizes and Wiltshire Gazette* 1858.
3 Bailey 2011.
4 Horowitz 2011, p.63. These ancillary services are not all directly, or indirectly, focused on reducing art crime. For example, Horowitz also includes in his figures insurers, shippers, handlers and interior designers.
5 Art Loss Register 2015.
6 Kreder 2007, pp 178–9, referring to a statement by Marc Masurovsky, co-founder of the Holocaust Art Restitution Project, quoted by Anna Schumann, 'Tech museum brings study of stolen art and law', *Daily Toreador* (Texas University student newspaper), 20 November 2006.
7 McNair and Hill 2008, p.209.
8 *Art Newspaper* 1997.
9 *Art Newspaper* 2001.

10 *Art Newspaper* 2004.
11 McShane 2007; Wittman 2011.
12 Jacobs 2013.
13 Charles Hill, 'Recovering stolen art: Practical recovery issues and the role of law enforcement agencies', in Palmer (ed.) 1998, p.177.
14 *Western Daily Press* 1877.
15 J.C. Smith, 'Rewards for the return of lost or stolen property: The civil and criminal law', in Palmer (ed.) 1998, p.173. Smith further notes that: 'Rewards were offered by the Home Office, by other public authorities, by insurance companies, committees of manufacturers, bodies of residents and by the individual victims.'
16 Theft Act 1968, available at: http://www.legislation.gov.uk/ukpga/1968/60.
17 Metropolitan Police Service press release, 'Solicitor jailed for stolen painting sale', July 2009, available at: http://content.met.police.uk/News/Solicitor-jailed-for-stolen-painting-sale/1260267534781/1257246745756. Three of the suspects received a 'not proven' verdict, while two received a 'not guilty' verdict.
18 Carrell March 2010; Carrell April 2010.
19 Interview with the author, April 2015.
20 An earlier reward of $250,000 was offered; the later reward payment from the total £3.5 million recovery costs was paid out for information that lead to the return of the two paintings.
21 Bailey 2011.
22 Associated Press 2013.
23 BBC News 2008.
24 Email conversation with the author, November 2015.
25 Renfrew 2000, p.20.
26 Interview with the author, December 2015.
27 http://artrecovery.com/DisputeResolution
28 http://www.lootedartcommission.com/Services
29 Weil 1981, p.4.
30 Roodt, 2013, p.289.
31 http://www.artcrimeresearch.org/ and http://www.ial.uk.com/
32 Interview with the author, March 2015.
33 Murphy 2009, p.4.
34 Genocchio 2008.
35 Adam 2014, p.93.
36 *ACA Galleries v. Kinney*, 2d 699 (S.D.NY).
37 Neuendorf 2015.
38 Pryor, February 2013. He was sentenced to 90 months in Federal Prison after having pleaded guilty.

39 Croft 2015.

40 *Hahn v. Duveen*, 234 N.Y.S. 185 (N.Y. Sup. Ct. 1929).

41 *McNally v. Yarnall*, no.90 Civ. 3076 (RWS), available at: http://www.leagle.com/decision/19911602764FSupp838_11455/McNALLY%20v.%20YARNALL. The case against the Metropolitan Museum was dismissed. The case as against James Yarnall was narrowed but a portion of it was to proceed to trial, however the case was later settled.

42 http://www.warholfoundation.org/legacy/authentication_procedure.html

43 For example, see *Kramer v. The Pollock-Krasner Found.*, 890 F. Supp. 250 (S.D.N.Y. 1995).

44 For further details, see: *Bilinski v. The Keith Haring Fndn.*, no.14-cv-1085-DLC slip op. (S.D.N.Y. 6 March 2015); aff'd by no.15-1121 slip op. (2d Cir. 2 December 2015).

45 Tarsis 2012.

46 http://www.axa-art.co.uk/artprotect.html.

47 For up-to-date information on this regulation and any recent changes, see http://www.sia.homeoffice.gov.uk

48 Further information available at http://www.legalservicesboard.org.uk/

49 Telephone conversation with the author, March 2015.

50 Gerlis June 2014.

51 Fairman 2014, p.17.

CHAPTER 5

1 The painting went missing from a London storeroom and was recovered in June 2007, as reported in BBC News 22 June 2007.

2 Stephens 2009.

3 The terms 'cultural heritage' and 'cultural property' are most commonly used when discussing law's interaction with the art world (i.e. rather than 'art' or 'antiques'). In keeping with the rest of this book, the terms 'cultural property', 'art' and 'cultural heritage' are used interchangeably within this chapter despite distinctions noted between the phrases.

4 Casini 2011, p.375.

5 http://portal.unesco.org/culture/es/ev.php-URL_ID=36292&URL_DO=DO_PRINTPAGE&URL_SECTION=201.html

6 Prowda 2013, p.14.

7 Janet Ulph, 'Criminal Offences Affecting the Trade in Art and Antiquities', in Ulph and Smith 2012, p.139.

8 *Accidia Foundation v. Simon Dickinson*, [2010] EWHC 3058 [CH]. It was later

decided that the agreement was void.

9 *Thome v. Alexander & Louisa Calder Foundation* (2009), available at: http://www.courts.state.ny.us/REPORTER/3dseries/2009/2009_08889.htm

10 Available at: https://www.icrc.org/ihl/INTRO/590

11 'UN Convention for Protection of Cultural Property in Event of Armed Conflict: Written question-1024', 3 June 2015, available at: http://www.parliament.uk/business/publications/written-questions-answers-statements/written-question/Commons/2015-06-03/1024/

12 Council Directive 93/7/EEC of 15 March 1993 on the return of cultural objects unlawfully removed from the territory of a Member State, available at: http://eur-lex.europa.eu/legal-content/EN/ALL/?uri=CELEX%3A31993L0007

13 Ministerial Advisory Panel on Illicit Trade 2000. The convention notes that this limitation period should generally be within 50 years of the theft or illicit excavation, and 3 years running from the victim's knowledge of its whereabouts. The government's earlier Select Committee had recommended the joining of UNIDROIT.

14 Merryman 1986.

15 Francesco Francioni, 'Plurality and interaction of legal orders in the enforcement of cultural heritage law', in Francioni and Gordley (eds) 2013, p.12.

16 *De Balkany v. Christie Manson and Woods Ltd* [1997], Q.B, TR.L.163.

17 BBC News 15 November 2010.

18 Competition Act 1998, available at: http://www.legislation.gov.uk/ukpga/1998/41/section/2.

19 Osborn and Kennedy 2002.

20 Erazmus 2015.

21 As noted and discussed in greater detail by Janet Ulph, 'Tracing and recovering stolen art or the proceeds of sale', in Palmer (ed.) 1998, p.101.

22 http://www.icaew.com/en/library/subject-gateways/law/money-laundering/uk-legislation-and-regulations

23 Janet Ulph, 'International Initiatives', in Ulph and Smith 2012, p.67.

24 The regulated sector as outlined by the Proceeds of Crime Act 2002, available at: http://www.legislation.gov.uk/uksi/2007/3287/made. The individual reporting the suspicious activity is the 'nominated officer': see sections 330–32 for further details:

25 Brodie March 2000; Lynch 1999.

26 The Treaty of Rome (signed in 1957) ensured members of the European Economic Community retained the right to keep cultural items, which they considered of significance, within their country.

27 For information on current agreements, see: http://eca.state.gov/cultural-heritage-center/cultural-property-protection/bilateral-agreements

28 The UK implemented it with its the Iraq (UN Sanctions) Order 2003, the US with an Emergency Protection for Iraqi Cultural Antiquities Act 2004.
29 Ruth Redmond-Cooper, 'Time limits in actions to recover stolen art', in Palmer (ed.) 1998, pp 148–9.
30 This led to the UK's Return of Cultural Objects Regulations 2004.
31 Patty Gerstenblith, 'Enforcement by domestic courts, criminal law and forfeiture in the recovery of cultural objects', in Francioni and Gordley 2013, p.171.
32 Vogel 1999.
33 *Vineberg v. Bissonnette*, 529 F.Supp.2d 300 (D.R.I. 2007); aff'd, 548 F.3d 50 (1st Cir. 2008).
34 713 F. Supp.2d 367 (S.D.N.Y. 2010), *Robin vs. Zwirner*, Craig Robins, no.10 CIV. 2787 (WHP). United States District Court, S.D. New York, 20 May 2010, *368. A settlement was later reached.
35 Dobrzynski 1998.
36 *William Foxley v. Sotheby's Inc.*, United States District Court, S.D. New York. 893 F.Supp. 1224 (1995). The court did allow the plaintiff's claims around breach of contract and a settlement between the parties was reached.
37 *Cowles v. Gagosian*, Supreme Court of the State of New York, County of New York, 2012 NY Slip Op 33156(U)
38 Kennedy 2012.
39 Dealing in Cultural Objects [Offences] Act (2003, available at: http://www.legislation.gov.uk/ukpga/2003/27/contents
40 Email conversation with the author, November 2015.
41 Select Committee on Culture, Media and Sport Seventh Report, paragraph 95, available at: http://www.parliament.the-stationery-office.co.uk/pa/cm199900/cmselect/cmcumeds/371/37106.htm
42 Simon Mackenzie, 'The market as criminal and criminals in the market: Reducing opportunities for organised crime in the international antiquities market', in Manacorda and Chappell (eds) 2011, p.71.
43 'Defence of due diligence', HC Deb 22 March 2001 vol.365 cc548-64, available at: http://hansard.millbanksystems.com/commons/2001/mar/22/defence-of-due-diligence#S6CV0365P0_20010322_HOC_406:
44 Ministerial Advisory Panel on Illicit Trade 2000, p.7.
45 Mellor 1997.
46 For further details, see: *Winkworth v. Christie Manson and Woods Ltd. and Another*, [1980] 1 ER (Ch) 496, [1980] 1 All ER 1121.
47 *United States v. McClain*, 551 F.2d 52, (5th Cir. 1977), 545 F.2d 988 (5th Cir. 1977), 593 F.2d 658 (5th Cir. 1979). United States v. McClain (McClain II) 593 f.2D 658 (5TH CIR 1979) cert denied 444 U.S. 918 (1979).

48 *United States v. Schultz*, 178 F.Supp 2d 445 (S.D.N.Y. 2002), aff'd, 333 F.3d (2d Cir. 2003), cert. denied, 540 U.S. 1106 (2004).

49 Prowda 2013, p.221, referring to, among others, A. James Casner and W. Barton Leach, *Cases and Text on Property*, 3rd edn, 1984, p.139.

50 Akinsha 2013.

51 Alessandro Checi, 'Plurality and coordination of dispute settlement methods in the field of cultural heritage', in Francioni and Gordley (eds) 2013, p.186.

52 Derek Fincham, 'Social norms and illicit cultural heritage', in Francioni and Gordley (eds) 2013, p.206.

CHAPTER 6

1 Conklin 1994, p.12.

2 Conklin 1994, p.96.

3 This is covered by the UK's Enterprise Act 2002 and the US's Sherman Act 1890.

4 Conklin 1994, p.102.

5 The case was well documented; details here from Glueck 1991.

6 Interview with the author, April 2014.

7 Interview with the author, April 2014.

8 Email conversation with the author, February 2015.

9 Thompson 2014, p.380.

10 Email conversation between the author and the FCA press team, November 2015.

11 http://www.cadellco.com/

12 Pryor July/August 2013.

13 News release by Autorité des Marchés Financiers, 21 February 2011. The investment company was later taken to court by the authority.

14 Linklaters newsletter, 'Regulatory Investigations Update', 1 April 2014, p.14, available at: http://www.linklaters.com/pdfs/mkt/london/April_Reg_Invests_FINAL.pdf

15 McAndrew 2011, p.13.

16 British Art Market Federation/Arts Economics 2015, p.11.

17 Telephone conversation with the author, February 2016.

18 Kuhn, 2014.

19 *Marguerite Hoffman v L&M Arts, et al.* United States District Court for the Northern District of Texas, Civil Action no.3:10-CV-0953-D (N.D. Tex. 15 August 2011). The plaintiff argued that the painting had been sold at a reduced price in return for discretion in relation to the sale. An initial trial found in

favour of Hoffman in 2013. A later US District Court released Martinez and his company from 'claims against them with prejudice' and reduced the amount due from L&M Arts.

20 Fontevecchia 2015.

21 Conversation with the author, March 2015.

22 Gerlis February 2014, p.18.

23 Pryor December 2012.

24 NSAF website: https://www.fbi.gov/about-us/investigate/vc_majorthefts/arttheft/national-stolen-art-file

25 Ministerial Advisory Panel on Illicit Trade 2000. The report also recommended a 'comprehensive and universally accessible database of international legislative information', p.35.

26 At this point the cost of a comprehensive database was estimated at £12 million over five years (CoPAT): http://www.publications.parliament.uk/pa/cm200304/cmselect/cmcumeds/59/5905.htm

27 The Assay Office monitors the system of hallmarks, which has its own legislation, the Hallmarking Act (1973). Conversation with author, November 2015.

28 www.statelyhomehotline.co.uk.

29 Email from the Art Loss Register to the author, November 2015.

30 Simon Mackenzie, 'The market as criminal and criminals in the market: Reducing opportunities for organised crime in the international antiquities market', in Manacorda and Chappell (eds) 2011, pp 69–86 (p.80).

31 Ministerial Advisory on Illicit Trade 2000, p.38.

32 Available at: http://tbamf.org.uk/wp-content/uploads/2014/08/BAMF-Anti-Money-Laundering-Guidelines-2016.pdf

33 Department for Culture, Media and Sport 2004, p.7.

34 As noted in Conklin 1994, p.257.

35 English Heritage, *Interventions: Prosecutions and Alternative Disposals*, May 2013, p.10.

36 Derek Fincham, 'Social norms and illicit cultural heritage', in Francioni and Gordley (eds) 2013, p.216.

37 Angeleti 2015. Kapoor is reported to have denied the allegations.

38 Brodie 1999.

CONCLUSION

1 Interview with the author, February 2015.

BIBLIOGRAPHY

Adam, Georgina, *Big Bucks: The Explosion of the Art Market in the 21st Century*, Lund Humphries, Farnham, 2014

Adam, Georgina and Pryor, Riah, 'The law vs scholarship', *Art Newspaper*, no.230, December 2011

Adams, Laurie, *Art Cop: Robert Volpe*, Dodd Mead & Company, New York, 1974

Akinsha, Konstantin, 'High court drama: Scholars, Christie's and the Russian Oligarch', Art News, 5 February 2013

Alder, Christine, 'Challenges to authenticity in the Aboriginal art market', paper presented at the 'Art Crime Protecting Art, Protecting Artists and Protecting Consumers Conference' convened by the Australian Institute of Criminology, Sydney, 2–3 December 1999

Angeleti, Gabriella, 'Flood of restitutions deepens as museums investigate objects bought through Subhash Kapoor', *Art Newspaper*, 21 October 2015

Art Loss Register, 'The first 25 years (1990–2015)', report

Art Newspaper, 'Hoary old fakes', *Art Newspaper*, 1 October 1991

Art Newspaper, 'Nordstern poach top detective from Scotland Yard', *Art Newspaper*, no.67, February 1997

Art Newspaper, 'The private sector must police itself', *Art Newspaper*, no.110, January 2001

Art Newspaper, 'New company will track stolen art', *Art Newspaper*, no.148, June 2004

Associated Press, 'Disputed Bulgarian dish fails at London auction', 12 February 2007

Associated Press, 'Dutch art heist paintings may have been burned by suspect's mother', *The Guardian*, 17 July 2013, available at: http://www.theguardian.com/artanddesign/2013/jul/17/dutch-art-heist-paintings-burned

Association of Chief Police Officers, 'Heritage and Cultural Property Crime National Policing Strategic Assessment', 2013

ATG Reporter, 'It's business as usual, says Freeport, as EU brings law change in Geneva', *Antiques Trade Gazette*, 28 September 2009

ATG Reporter, 'Chinese art market concerns raise question of regulation',

Antiques Trade Gazette, 5 November 2012

Bailey, Martin, 'My life as an undercover negotiator', *Art Newspaper*, no.226, 1 July 2011

Baumel, Jacques, 'The destruction by war of the cultural heritage in Croatia and Bosnia-Herzegovina', Committee on Culture and Education, Information report, Doc 6756, 2 February 1993

Bazley, Thomas D., *Crimes of the Art World*, Praeger, Santa Barbara, California, 2010

BBC News, 'Looted art returned to Afghanistan', 19 July 2012

BBC News, 'Amarna Princess statue to return to Bolton Museum', 15 November 2010

BBC News, 'Stolen paintings found in Zurich', 19 February 2008

BBC News, 'Historic archive theft man fined', 13 May 2008

BBC News, 'Stolen bronze sculpture recovered', 26 July 2007

BBC News, 'Missing Magritte painting located', 22 June 2007

Beech, Hannah, 'Spirited away', *Time*, 13 October 2003

Binnie, Isla, 'Police seize possible Leonardo da Vinci in Switzerland', Reuters, 11 February 2015

Boroff, Philip and Freifeld, Karen, 'Distraught Salander, sentenced to up to 18 years, says sorry', Bloomberg Business, 4 August 2010

Branigan, Tania, 'Chinese bidder refuses to pay for Yves Saint Laurent-owned artefacts', *The Guardian*, 2 March 2009

British Art Market Federation/Arts Economics, 'The British art market in 2014', 2015

Brodie, Neil, Doole, Jenny and Watson, Peter, *Stealing History: The Illicit Trade in Cultural Material*, The McDonald Institute for Archaeological Research, Cambridge, 2000

Brodie, Neil, 'The concept of due dilligence and the antiquities trade', March 2000

Brodie, Neil, 'Book review: Katie Demakopoulou & Nicoleta Divari-Valakou, 1997, *The Aidonia Treasure*', Illicit Antiquities Research Centre, July 1999

Campbell, Jon, 'Bharara orders banker's Basquiat back to Brazil', *Village Voice*, 25 June 2015

Carrell, Severin, 'The great Leonardo da Vinci heist: Solicitor accused of £4m extortion plot', *The Guardian*, 1 March 2010,

Carrell, Severin, 'Five cleared of trying to extort £4.25m from duke over stolen Da Vinci painting', *The Guardian*, 21 April 2010

Casini, Lorenzo, 'Italian Hours: The globalisation of cultural property law', *International Journal of Constitutional Law*, vol.9, no.2, 2011, pp 369–93

Chappell, Duncan and Hufnagel, Saskia (eds), *Contemporary Perspectives on the*

Detection, Investigation and Prosecution of Art Crime, Ashgate, Farnham, 2014
Charney, Noah, *Art and Crime: Exploring the Dark Side of the Art World*, Praeger, Santa Barbara, California, 2009
Chicago Tribune, 'Stolen Picasso found at drug lord's house', *Chicago Tribune*, 10 April 2005
Christie's press release, 'Christie's International sets a new house record for the most expensive item sold online', 28 November 2012
Commission for Looted Art in Europe, 'Introduction to the National Archives' records on Nazi-era looted cultural property, 1939–1961', undated
Committee for Cultural Policy, 'Indian statues return to resolve diplomatic spat', 13 January 2014
Conklin, John. E, *Art Crime*, Praeger, Westport, Connecticut, 1994
Coomber, Jarrett, 'A quantitative study of the economic effects of art theft on art prices and returns', Master's thesis, Erasmus School of History, Culture and Communication, Erasmus University, Rotterdam, 2013
Croft, Jane, 'Judge backs Sotheby's in Caravaggio legal battle', *Financial Times*, 16 January 2015
D'Arcy, Scott, 'Gang found guilty of £800,000 fraud after being caught out by Highworth auction house', *Swindon Advertiser*, 27 February 2013
Davis, Tess, 'Supply and demand: Exposing the illicit trade in Cambodian antiquities through a study of Sotheby's auction house', *Crime, Law and Social Change*, vol.56, no.2, July 2011, pp 155–74
Department for Culture, Media and Sport, 'The 1970 UNESCO Convention: Guidance for dealers and auctioneers in cultural property', January 2004
Department of Justice, 'Auction house and company's president plead guilty to wildlife smuggling conspiracy', 14 January 2015
Devizes and Wiltshire Gazette, 'Recovery of the Earl of Suffolk's paintings', 11 February 1858
Dobrzynski, Judith H., 'A betrayal the art world can't forget: The battle for Rothko's estate altered lives and reputations', *New York Times*, 2 November 1998
Doland, Angela, 'China's art market stumbles', *The Financialist*, 20 March 2013
Durney, Mark, 'Art theft statistics: Valuable tools in need of reliable measures', *American Society of International Law Cultural Heritage and Arts Review*, Autumn/Winter 2010, pp 13–16
Durney, Mark, 'Reevaluating art crime's famous figures', *International Journal of Cultural Property*, vol.20, no.2, May 2013, pp 221–32
Dutra, Michael, 'Sir, how much is that Ming vase in the window?', 2004
Efrat, Asif, 'Protecting against plunder, the United States and the international efforts', Cornell Law Faculty Working Papers, February 2009

English Heritage, *A Guide for Owners, Tenants and Managers of Heritage Assets*, May 2013

English Heritage, *Interventions: Prosecution and alternative disposals*, May 2013

Erazmus, Dominika, 'On this day in 1914: Suffragette Mary Richards slashes National Gallery painting', Museum of London, 4 March 2015

Esterow, Milton, 'The 10 most faked artists', 6 January 2005

European Commission, 'Fighting organised crime in the Balkans', IP/03/1608, Brussels, 26 November 2003

Evans, Stephen, 'Cornelius Gurlitt: One lonely man and his hoard of stolen Nazi art', BBC News, 26 March 2014

Fairman, Darlene, 'The true cost of authentication litigation', *Art & Advocacy*, vol.15, Spring/Summer 2013, pp 10–11

Feroozi, Abdul Wasey, 'The impact of war upon Afghanistan's cultural heritage', Archaeological Institute of America, March 2004

Francioni, Francesco and Gordley, James (eds), *Enforcing International Cultural Heritage Law*, Oxford University Press, Oxford, 2013

Frulli, Micaela, 'Advancing the protection of cultural property through the implementation of individual criminal responsibility: The case-law of international criminal tribunal for the former Yugoslavia', *Italian Yearbook of International Law*, vol.15, no.1, 2005, pp 195–216

Fontevecchia, Agustino, 'Steve Cohen's Modigliani in the middle of an art market war: Billionaire Rybolovlev vs Yves Bouvier', *Forbes*, 12 March 2015

Gapper, John and Aspden, Peter, 'Davos 2015: Nouriel Roubini says art market needs regulation', *Financial Times*, 22 January 2015

Genocchio, Benjamin, 'Seized, reclaimed and now on view', *New York Times*, 27 April 2008

Gerlis, Melanie, *Art as an Investment?*, Lund Humphries, Farnham, February 2014

Gerlis, Melanie, 'The rise of the art adviser', *Art Newspaper*, Art Basel daily edition, June 2014

Gill, Charlotte and Hull, Liz, 'The artful codgers: Pensioners who conned British museums with £10m forgeries', *Daily Mail*, 16 November 2007

Gill, David, 'Context matters: Looting in the Balkans', *Journal of Art Crime*, no.63, Autumn 2009, pp 63–6

Glueck, Grace, 'Mistrust at hearing on art regulation', *New York Times*, 31 January 1991

Gordon, Lorna, 'Tracey Emin forgery artist Jonathan Rayfern jailed', 28 October 2010

Gruber, Stefan, 'Perspectives on the investigation, prosecution and prevention of crime in Asia'

Guo, Jia, 'What drives the Chinese art market? The case of elegant bribery', undated

Harrington, Spencer P.M., 'Chinese thieves executed, but loot remains at large', Archaeological Institute of America online, 2 February 2000

Hill, Charles, 'Art crime and the Wealth of Nations', *Journal of Financial Crime*, vol.15, no.4, 2008, pp 444–8

Hirst, David, 'Report of the Spoliation Panel in respect of an oil sketch by Sir Peter Paul Rubens "The Coronation of the Virgin", now in possession of the Samuel Courtauld Trust', The Stationery Office, London, 15 December 2010

Hiscox report, 'Online Art Trade Report 2014'

Historic England and ARCH (Alliance to Reduce Crimes against Heritage), 'Heritage Crime: Guidance for Sentencers', undated

Historic England, 'Heritage Crime Impact Statements', May 2013

Horowitz, Noah, *Art of the Deal*, Princeton University Press, Princeton, New Jersey, 2011

Hufnagel, Saskia Dr and Chappell, Duncan, *Contemporary Perspectives on the Detection, Investigation and Prosecution of Art Crime: Australasian, European and North American Perspectives*, Ashgate, Farnham, October 2014

International Foundation for Art Research, Educational Resources/Art Law and Cultural Property – for numerous case papers and summaries throughout the book

Jacobs, Emma, 'Lessons from an old master', *Financial Times*, 23 May 2013

Jones, Jonathan, 'Scandal in China over the museum with 40,000 fake artefacts', *The Guardian*, 17 July 2013a

Jones, Mark (ed.), *Why Fakes Matter*, British Museum Press, London, 1992

Karczewski, Lisa A. (Fox Rothschild LLP), 'Authenticating art with bioengineered DNA: The IP issues', 2 November 2015

Kessenides, Elizabeth, 'Fakes, mistakes and income tax deductions', *Spencers Art Lawy Journal*, vol.1, no.2, September/October 2010

Keating, Fiona, 'Priceless ancient relics looted by Isis in Iraq and Syria sold on eBay', *International Business Times*, 14 March 2015

Kennedy, Randy, 'Gagosian suit offers rare look at art dealing', *New York Times*, 7 November 2012

Keohane, David, 'China vs the so-called art industry', *Financial Times*, 29 January 2015

Kreder, Jennifer Anglim, 'Reconciling individual and group justice with the need for repose in Nazi-looted art disputes', *Brooklyn Law Review*, vol.73, December 2007, pp 155–216

Kuhn, Stephan, 'A delicate balance', *Tax Insights for Business Leaders*, no.12, 2014, p.3

Lemerick, 'Fakes for Rich Tourists', *The Derby Daily Telegraph*, 28 July 1928, available from the British Newspaper Archive

Lewis, Danny, 'How "Operation Mummy's Curse" is helping fight terrorism', *Smithsonian*, 28 April 2015

Liverpool Mercury, 'Faked antiquities', 26 December 1895, available at the British Newspaper Archive

Lynch, M., 'Priceless stolen Greek antiquities found in fish crate', *Miami Herald*, 15 September 1999

Mackenzie, S.R.M., *Going, Going, Gone: Regulating the Market in Illicit Antiquities*, Institute of Art and Law, Leicester, 2005

Mackenzie, Simon and Green, Penny, 'Criminalising the Market in Illicit Antiquities', ESRC-funded survey published in *Criminology and Archaeology: Studies in Looted Antiquities*, Oñati International Series in Law and Society, Hart Publishing, Oxford, 2009, pp 145–70

Manacorda, Stefano (ed.), *Selected papers and contributions from the International Conference on 'Organised crime in art and antiquities', Courmayeur Mont Blanc, Italy, 12–14 December 2008*, International Scientific and Professional Advisory Council of the United Nations Crime Prevention and Criminal Justice Programme, 2009

Manacorda, Stefano and Chappell, Duncan (eds), *Crime in the Art and Antiquities World*, Springer, New York, 2011

Martinez, Alanna, 'World art market booms to record $54 billion as US uber-wealthy fuel growth', *The Observer*, 3 November 2015

McAndrew, Clare, *Fine Art and High Finance: Expert Advice on the Economics of Ownership*, Bloomberg Press, New York, January 2010

McAndrew, Clare, 'The role of art & antique dealers: an added value', prepared for CINOA, 2011

McAndrew, Clare, 'The International Art Market, in 2011: Observations of the art trade over 25 years', TEFAF, Maastricht, 2012

McAndrew, Clare, 'TEFAF Art Market Report 2015', TEFAF, Maastricht, 2015

McAndrew, Clare, 'TEFAF Art Market Report', TEFAF, Maastricht, 2015

McNair, Clarissa and Hill, Charles, 'Art and crime', in Iain Robertson and Derrick Chong (eds), *The Art Business*, Routledge, Abingdon, Oxfordshire and New York, 2008, pp 197–210

McShane, Thomas, 'Loot: Inside the World of Stolen Art', Maverick House, Dunshaughlin, Co. Meath, 2007

Mellor, James, 'Egyptian treasures smuggler is jailed', *Independent*, 19 June 1997

Merryman, John Henry, 'Two ways of thinking about cultural property', *American Journal of International Law*, vol.80, no.4, October 1986, pp 831–53

Merryman John Henry, *Thinking about the Elgin Marbles: Critical Essays on*

Cultural Property, Art and Law, Kluwer Law International, Alphen aan den Rijn, 2000

Metropolitan Police Service, 'Solicitor jailed for stolen painting sale', press release, 2 July 2009

Milliard, Coline, 'Art dealer Guy Wildenstein caught up in €600 million tax evasion case', 18 September 2014

Ministerial Advisory Panel on Illicit Trade, 'Report', Department for Culture, Media and Sport, London, December 2000

Morpeth Herald, 'Strange recovery of stolen property', 13 February 1858, available at the British Newspaper Archive

Mowat, Ian, 'The Revival of the National and University Library of Bosnia and Herzegovina in Sarajevo: A study of options and proposals for action', UNESCO, 1994

Murphy, Nathan, 'Splitting images: Shared-value settlements in Nazi-era art restitution claims', *Florida Entertainment Law Review*, vol.3, 2009, pp 41–79

MutualArt staff, 'Stealing the spotlight: Art thefts of 2011', Huffpost Arts, 15 October 2011

Neuendorf, Henri, 'Found guilty of fraud, art advisor Helge Achenbach sentenced to six years in prison', artnet news, 16 March 2015

Noce, Vincent, 'Siamese crown stolen from Château de Fontainebleau', Art Newspaper online, 2 March 2015

Norman, Geraldine, 'What Interpol wants for Christmas', *Independent*, 22 December 1996

Office for National Statistics, 'Crime statistics, focus on public perceptions of crime and the police and the personal well-being of victims, 2013 to 2014', 26 March 2015

Osborn, Andrew and Kennedy, Maev, 'Sotheby's fined £13m for price-fixing scandal with Christie's', *The Guardian*, 31 October 2002

Oster, Shai, 'German held on art smuggling in China as buyers dodge tax', Bloomberg Business, 16 May 2012

Palmer, Norman (ed.), *The Recovery of Stolen Art: A Collection of Essays*, Kluwer Law International, London, 1998

Parry, Roland Lloyd (Agence France-Presse), 'Gao Ping, Chinese high-flyer busted in Spain', InterAksyon.com, 20 October 2012

Parsons, Ben, 'Police warning against Brighton antiques firm', *The Argus*, 30 June 2011

Pears, Elizabeth, 'Forty Hall Museum thief jailed for "robbing Britain's heritage"', *Enfield Independent*, 26 January 2011

Petrovic, Jadranka, *The Old Bridge of Mostar and Increasing Respect for Cultural Property in Armed Conflict*, Martinus Nijhoff, Leiden, 2013

Pogrebin, Robin and Flynn, Kevin, 'As art values rise, so do concerns about market's oversight', *New York Times*, 27 January 2013

Popper, Nathaniel, 'Top lawyer on Holocaust restitution cases taking flak over fee request', *The Forward*, 13 January 2006

Prince, Dominic, 'Where's the money for our masterpieces? Fine art world is rocked as top Mayfair dealer is sued by his clients over missing millions', *Daily Mail*, 5 July 2015

Prowda, Judith B., *Visual Arts and the Law: A Handbook for Professionals*, Lund Humphries, Farnham, 2013

Pryor, Riah, 'Could do better? The hunt for missing government art', *Art Newspaper*, no.228, September 2011

Pryor, Riah, 'Balkans targeted in hunt for stolen art', *Art Newspaper*, no.231, January 2012

Pryor, Riah, 'Victims of forgery are "left in limbo"', *Art Newspaper*, no.238, September 2012

Pryor, Riah, 'Court rules auction houses should be more transparent', *Art Newspaper*, no.241, December 2012, section 2, p.5

Pryor, Riah, 'Growth in internet sales forces fraud issue', *Art Newspaper*, no.242, January 2013

Pryor, Riah, 'Gauguin in alleged fraud by former NFL star', *Art Newspaper*, no.243, February 2013

Pryor, Riah, 'How to stop a thief', *Art Newspaper*, no.243, February 2013, available at: http://old.theartnewspaper.com/articles/How-to-stop-a-thief/28548

Pryor, Riah, 'UK tightens rules on art funds', *Art Newspaper*, no.248, July/August 20133

Pryor, Riah and Gerlis, Melanie, 'Sotheby's calls on author to retract looted art report', *Art Newspaper*, no.228, September 2011, p.75

Radosavljevic, Zoran, 'Croatia's ex-PM, biggest party sentenced over slush funds', Reuters, 11 March 2014

Renfrew, Colin, *Loot, Legitimacy and Ownership*, Gerald Duckworth & Co., London, 2000

Reuters, 'China seizes $14.5bn assets from Zhou Yongkang family and associates –report', *The Telegraph*, 30 March 2014

Reuters Warsaw, 'Pole and German claim to have found missing Nazi loot train', *The Guardian*, 19 August 2015

Riedlmayer, András, 'Killing memory: The targeting of Bosnia's cultural heritage', testimony presented at a hearing of the Commission on Security and Cooperation in Europe, US Congress, 4 April 1995

Riedlmayer, András J., 'From the ashes: The past and future of Bosnia's cultural heritage', in Maya Shatzmiller (ed.), 'Islam and Bosnia: Conflict Resolution and Foreign Policy in Multi-Ethnic States, McGill-Queens University Press, Montreal, 2002, pp 98–135

Riedlmayer, András J., 'Crimes of war, crimes of peace: Destruction of libraries during and after the Balkan Wars of the 1990s', *Library Trends*, vol.56, no.1, Summer 2007, pp 107–32

Robertson, Iain, video interview, available at: http://www.sothebys.com

Robertson, Iain and Chong, Derrick (eds), *The Art Business*, Routledge, London and New York, 2008

Rogoff, Kenneth, 'The Art of Capital Flight', Business Standard, 16 September 2015

Roodt, Christa, 'Restitution of art and cultural objects and its limits', *Comparative and International Law Journal of Southern Africa*, vol.46, 2013, pp 286–307

Salisbury, Laney and Sujo, Aly, *The Conman: How One Man Fooled The Modern Art Establishment*, Gibson Square Books, London, 2010

Sandipan, Urmil, *Cultural Property Law, Management, Protection and Preservation of Heritage*, Regal Publications, New Delhi, 2013

Sevenoaks Chronicle and Kentish Advertiser, 'Frauds in art', 3 February 1899, available from the British Newspaper Archive

Scheerhout, John, 'Guilty: £1.7m Lowry robber', *Manchester Evening News*, 19 February 2009

Shabi, Rachel, 'Looted in Syria – and sold in London: The British antiques shops dealing in artefacts smuggled by ISIS', *The Guardian*, 3 July 2015

Shaheen, Kareem, 'Isis fighters destroy ancient artefacts at Mosul Museum', *The Guardian*, 26 February 2015

Spiegel online, 'Spiegel interview with Wolfgang Beltracchi: Confessions of a genius art forger', 9 March 2012

Stephens, Mark, 'The police came tromping into Tate Modern as nosy parkers', *Art Newspaper*, no.208, December 2009

Tarsis, Irina, 'The Keith Haring Foundation announces its decision to disband authentication committee', 20 September 2012

Telegraph, 'John Hobbs: Obituary', *The Telegraph*, 15 April 2011

Thompson, Erin, 'Successes and failures of self-regulatory regimes governing museum holdings of Nazi-looted art and looted antiquities', *Columbia Journal of Law and the Arts*, vol.37, July 2014, pp 379–404

Tijhuis, A.J.G., *Transnational Crime and the Interface between Legal and Illegal Actors: The Case of the Illicit Art and Antiques Trade*, Wolf Legal Publishers, Nijmegen, 2006

Tribble, Jennifer, 'Antiquities trafficking and terrorism: Where cultural wealth, political violence, and criminal networks intersect', The Monterey Terrorism Research and Education Program, 2014

Tyler, Jane, 'Police arrest 13 men over thefts from museums and galleries', *Birmingham Mail*, 6 November 2014

Ulph, Janet and Smith, Ian, *The Illicit Trade in Art and Antiquities*, Hart Publishing, Oxford, 2012

UNESCO, 'The fight against the illicit trafficking of cultural objects', March 2011

UNESCO, 'Director-General Irina Bokova firmly condemns the destruction of Palmyra's ancient temple of Baalshamin, Syria', 2015 (undated)

United States Sentencing Commission, memo to Senators Leahy & Hatch, 'Penalties for Cultural Heritage Resources', 3 April 2002

US Attorney's Office

Valentin, Pierre, 'The destruction of fakes', 12 September 2013

Van der Auwera, Sigrid, 'Unesco and the protection of cultural property during armed conflict', *International Journal of Cultural Policy*, vol.19, no.1, 2013, pp 1–19

Vitelli, Karen D., 'Looting and theft of cultural property: Are we making progress?', Getty Conservation Institute, Newsletter 15.1, Spring 2000

Vogel, Carol, 'Austrian Rothschilds decide to sell: Sotheby's in London will auction $40 million in art seized by Nazis', *New York Times*, 10 April 1999

Walton, Kenneth, *Fake: Forgery, Lies, & eBay*, Simon Spotlight Entertainment, New York, 2007

Watson, Peter and Todeschini, Cecilia, *The Medici Conspiracy*, Public Affairs US, New York, 2006

Webb, Jonathan, *Stolen: The Gallery of Missing Masterpieces*, Herbert Press, London, 2008

Weil, Stephen E, 'Some thoughts on "Art Law"', *Dickinson Law Review*, vol.85, no.4, 1981, pp 555–63

Western Daily Press, 'Recovery of the Stolen Van Eyck', *Western Daily Press*, 5 April 1877

Williams, Matthew, *Virtually Criminal: Crime, Deviance and Regulation Online*, Routledge, London, 2006

Withers Worldwide, 'Public register on EU trusts?', 12 February 2014

Wittman, Robert, 'The FBI Art Theft Program and its impact on collecting: A report from FBI Special Agent Robert Wittman and the editor', *American Society of Arms Collectors Bulletin*, no.93, 2005

Wittman, Robert, *Priceless: How I Went Undercover to Rescue the World's Stolen Treasures*, Broadway Books, New York, June 2011

Zimonjic, Vesna Peric, 'Govt returns looted arts to Croatia', Inter Press Service News Agency, 20 December 2001

INDEX

Note: Page numbers followed by *n* refer to information in a note.